How to Paint & Draw Motorcycles

Eric Herrmann

Published by:
Wolfgang Publications Inc.
217 Second Street North
Stillwater, MN 55082
http://www.wolfgangpublications.com

Legals

First published in 2004 by Wolfgang Publications Inc.,
217 Second Street North, Stillwater MN 55082

ISBN number: 1-929133-16-2

Printed and bound in the USA

How to Paint & Draw Motorcycles

Dedication

To the two women

in my life,

Mom

and

my very supportive

wife

Suzanne.

Introduction

What a project. When Tim from Wolfgang Publications and I got together on this book I thought cool, a book. I'll never read another book or magazine without appreciating how much work goes in to it. The one thing it did do for me was make me realize where the last fifteen years went. I guess I actually did something over that period of time. I'm not a writer, I went to art school. I did try to jot down some of the thoughts and processes that go through an artistic mind. I like to think I'm a normal guy just like everyone else. But I guess I see things in an artistic light just as an engineer would look at a structure and analyze it in their own technical perspective. I love bikes and I love to paint. I hope I might just inspire one reader to go for a ride or pick up a paint brush and begin painting. Thanks to all my motorcycle industry friends that have made my career so enjoyable. Maybe I'll write another one, in about fifteen years. I hope to see you all down the road.

www.EricHerrmannStudios.com

Hanging in my studio with a recently completed work. After three months of working on a painting, it's a great feeling of accomplishment.

Chapter One

Who Is Eric Herrmann?

Evolution of an Artist

Most kids like to draw. I just never gave it up. Or never grew up. My art and motorcycles are the two constants that have been with me for a very long time. I won the first art contest I can remember when I was in fourth grade. I've been painting and drawing ever since. I won my first motorcycle in a contest when I was twelve years old. I've been riding ever since. It all

One of my first professional art showings where I was painting on location. Early works started out as landscapes and vehicles, with my first motorcycle painting in the corner of the photograph titled "Cowboy & Indian."

makes sense now. I'm a motorcycle artist doing the two things I enjoy and am good at, riding and painting.

When you were in grade school there was always a kid that could draw anything. That was me. I was always getting in trouble for drawing T-bucket hot rods and Big Daddy Rat cartoons when I should have been doing my math homework. The funny thing was I didn't think I was all that good at art. People frequently ask me "You must have been born with that talent weren't you?" Maybe I had some degree of artistic talent, but I believe that if I would have stopped drawing and didn't get a formal art education I would not be an artist today. It's like any skill. If you keep at it your whole life you

had better improve or you need to find another profession. I'm a firm believer in both college education, and on the job skills, which have honed my artistic and thought abilities to where I am at currently. I also feel my art is just beginning and am anxious to see what I can do over the next twenty years.

While I didn't plan my career as an artist it's evident now that's what I was born to do. When I was in grade school I got a job cleaning the office of the local paper two nights a week so I could be around their art room and learn about layout and paste up. By high school I was working for an uncle who was the general manager of a chain of newspapers. I was working around the newspaper industry and high speed web

Exhibiting at the prestigious Barrett-Jackson Auto Auction in 1993, I sold two motorcycle paintings and received a commission for a third work while selling none of my car paintings.

presses. During the early years of college I was an apprentice sign painter and learned how to pin stripe, letter, and honed my skills with a brush. This education and development of skills now seems as important as the concepts of color and design I learned about in college. Thanks Mom.

Painting motorcycles and mechanical objects also seems like it developed as a product of my environment. I grew up in Chicago, a very blue collar town, where my mother and father owned a machinery business. My three older brothers were all gear heads and the neighbors used to call our street gasoline alley. I remember taking a count at one time and we had seven cars, three bikes, and two boats parked at our small suburban home. Brother Bob was a drag racer, Carl was a sports car fanatic, Dick still collects Corvettes, and I was the biker.

I won my first motorcycle in a contest when I was in eighth grade and I can't even count how many bikes I've had since then. From dirt bikes to café racers, crotch rockets, hand built

The first painting I put in to print "Time Out" still remains a seller in my catalog. The original sold in 1994 for $1500 and was resold in 1999 for around $10,000.

customs by Jesse James and Harold Pontarelli, I've had and enjoyed them all. I currently own five motorcycles, although that changes almost daily, ride on both the street and the dirt, and am considering some desert racing in the near future. All of my early influences involved motor sports of one form or another. My father was interested in sports one day a year when The Indianapolis 500 was running. A number of years later I was selected as the official artist for Indy. Thanks Dad.

In High School I was one of only three guys who took art. All the rest of my buddies were taking shop classes. When it came time to graduate and go to college, art school was my only consideration. I attended Triton College of Fine Art, a junior college, and took several classes at The Art Institute of Chicago as well. At Triton, illustration instructor Bob O'Malley took me under his wing and steered me in the right direction. Man that guy could paint. Bob was friends with a then up and coming artist name Leroy Neiman. I aced all my classes because I was a good artist and Bob suggested I attend The Art Center College of Design. The Art Center is famous for Automotive and Industrial design and Willie G. Davidson is one of their graduates. I submitted my portfolio, confident that I would get accepted. Big let down, I didn't get in. With my bubble totally burst I spent the next two years driving a truck and working at night as a bouncer in a disco. I made some good

The Big Time - a corporate sponsor builds a semi to transport and display my artwork around the country.

money over the next two years and had some awesome bikes, but I didn't do much artwork and it was getting to me.

This was a tough decision but probably one of the best of my life. I had to get out of Chicago and get back to creating art. I sold the bike and all my possessions, accumulated the mass sum of $800.00, and headed for Arizona where I was accepted at Arizona State University School of Art. I spent the next four years at ASU studying graphic design, painting, printing technologies, and the fine art of partying. I excelled at all. Most of this time I only had a motorcycle and didn't even own a car. I carried my brushes and paints on the back of my bike and pin striped cars and bikes for dealerships and bike clubs. I created logos for companies, signs for small restaurants, drawings for

Riding my Harold Pontarelli built softail through the desert near my home - one of my favorite things to do.

11

Mike, Lisa, (my spokes-model) and Kenny from Samson Exhaust at Biketoberfest.

Willie G. Davidson signing one of my prints at a charity auction during bike week.

t-shirt designs and got by using my artistic talents. It's not like I was making big bucks but it was better than flipping hamburgers to get through school. It also taught me the art of business and what I had to do to make a living with my artwork.

Towards the end of college at ASU I got hooked up with a friend that was running a t-shirt screen-printing operation from his apartment. His girl friend was doing the artwork, skateboard and surfing stuff, and John was selling the clothing to shops in Arizona and southern California. The chick split and John got a hold of me to do the artwork. Then John splits and I've got this small home run operation and a bunch of accounts. Upon graduating college I sought out an investor and opened my first legitimate business - Nitro Graphics, an art and screen print operation. Over the next eight long years, I bought out my partner, expanded to twelve employees, met my wife, and learned about business

In the year 2000 I was asked to create a motorcycle painting to commemorate the Indianapolis 500. It was quite a memorable experience, and a canvas print of the original now hangs in their museum.

the hard way. Suzanne and I bought a house, had our first son Ian, and I was wearing suits to work and schmoozing corporate accounts. I was getting further and further away from my art-

work and was now hiring staff artists. I was a businessman and I hated it.

Ian was two years old, Suzanne was pregnant with second son Dustin, and I was turning into a cranky businessman. This was probably also due to the fact that it was the only period in my life I didn't have my own motorcycle. I was in my thirties and decided I wanted to paint full time and try to make a living as an artist. With an incredibly understanding wife and some freaked out in-laws, we sold the business so I could pursue my painting career. I had a small income from payments on the business but it wasn't enough to make it. We rolled the dice and I started to do some art shows. At this time I was painting southwestern scenes because I thought that's what I needed to do to support my family. I was painting and that was better suited to me

Daytona Bike Week 2004, working on a painting for Baker Drivetrain, wearing my Hamster colors.

than being in business, but I still didn't get it. Finally we had a professional artist friend over to dinner and he said, "Eric, you've got to paint what you know." Following his recommendation I started to paint some large-scale motorcycles and cars on canvas. I even got my paintings into a prestigious Scottsdale art gallery. I still wasn't making enough to support the family.

Since I was a kid I always wanted to design my own home. It took Suzanne and I four years but we finally got it finished.

In 1993 I got the attention of the Barrett-Jackson folks, the world-renowned car auction. With a painting of an old Packard I became the official artist that year. My display at Barrett-Jackson consisted of a number of car paintings and two motorcycle paintings. At this prestigious car show I sold both bike paintings, got a commission to do a third motorcycle work, and didn't move any car art. It didn't take me long to figure this one out, I was painting bikes. There also wasn't any motorcycle art available at the time. Dave Mann, the original biker artist, was doing illustrations for Easyriders,

Ian, Dustin, Suzanne, and Eric. The family that rides together stays together. As my kids get older they seem to know everything, but I can still teach them a thing or two out on the track.

but there was no fine art to speak of. My paintings were nowhere near the price they are today. I would take whatever I could get, $1000 to $1500 and I was happy. My motorcycle art career was beginning and I decided to hit the road. While having art in a gallery was good for the ego, it didn't make me any money. Galleries will take 50 to 60% commission and you normally don't get bikers going through an art gallery. Suzanne stayed home with the two young sons, working a job as well, while I headed to Harley's 90th Anniversary. We struggled in those years but my paintings started to sell. Often I'd move a painting so I could get gas money to get home. I learned more about the motorcycle industry, exhibited with H.O.G. for

several years, and started traveling to all the events to promote my artwork. While these were challenging times they were also fun. The people I work with now at the bike magazines, famous motorcycle builders and manufacturers, were all getting started as well. When I was in LA there was always a floor to crash on. We all shared expenses, slept in trucks and campgrounds, and made it to the next motorcycle rally. I formed friendships in the motorcycle industry that will last a lifetime.

Attending all the bike events, I realized in a very short time, only a select few individuals would have the capabilities to purchase an original painting. I needed to reproduce my paintings as prints and get them to an affordable

The new studio is almost finished! Hidden in the hills with my motorcycles and my art. I've worked a lifetime for this.

price range so everyone could enjoy them. This was not only a financial move but a marketing tool as well. The more images you get out on the street with your name on them the more recognition you'll get. Every time I sold a painting I would take the profits and produce one of my paintings as a print edition. This didn't leave me with much money, but over the years I have built up an inventory of prints and now have over thirty of my original paintings reproduced as prints. As with any business, I continually invest back in to my artwork. I've developed a line of glass sculptures, a t-shirt line, note cards, and now a book. It's been a long road, but my art has sold in over forty countries and I feel like I'm just beginning to paint bikes. I enjoy the bike events, the camaraderie, riding my bikes, and especially painting. You need to take care of business and make a profit but it's still all about the art. If I feel the need to go riding, or don't answer the phone because I'm painting, I may miss a sale. That's the way it goes. Leave a number and I'll call you back. If you're a biker you'll understand.

Thirty five years ago I started out racing dirt bikes. The crashes hurt more and the jumps aren't as high as they used to be, but it's still one of my favorite forms of motorcycling.

If I don't answer the phone, maybe it's because I'm hangin' out with friends at the Hideaway, the local biker bar just down the road from our new house.

At home in my old studio with my paintings and bikes around. The only thing better would be a bigger studio with more bikes and paintings.

Chapter Two

The Studio

Creative Space

Every aspiring artist dreams of having a cool studio that you can hang out in and be creative. The only way you will ever get that studio is by creating artwork in the garage, dining room, spare bedroom, or whatever space you have at the time. I've heard more excuses from artist wannabees that I don't have the room, my lighting's not correct, or I have to be in the mood to paint, what a crock. After years of painting wherever I could, I'm finally building my own separate studio space. I highly doubt my artwork will be any better or worse because of it. While the tools and lighting will help, don't use it as an excuse not to create. If you are an artist you are always in the mood to paint and you should be able to do it anytime, anywhere.

While I now have several nice easels, for years I used what is called grid wall. It's a type of wire grid used for display purposes and you can attach different pegs and brackets easily. Total cost was about fifty bucks. All you need to do is move your painting up and down to get to the areas you need to paint. If I'm on the road and I want to paint, an easel can be fabricated out of just about anything. A table or chair, a chair on top of a table, they are all just tools and won't make your artwork any better, just easier. Just start painting. You'll eventually get all the cool studio stuff.

Lighting is important in your working environment but can come from many sources. As a matter of fact, I prefer lighting to come from sev-

Putting the finishing touches on a work is an exciting moment. It's a project that you have worked on for many months, starting out with only a concept it's now become a reality.

eral different sources. If I can get a combination of daylight, bright light bulbs, and fluorescent light, that's what I prefer. I currently have track lights mounted five feet back from the wall where my easels are located so I can position the lights on my painting. I also have an artists lamp that has a fluorescent and white bulb that rolls and I can position it where needed. I wouldn't say my lighting is color correct by any means, but I've gotten accustomed to painting just about anywhere. As I

get older the lighting is becoming more important.

Distractions in the studio will be different for everyone. As my studio has been in my home for years while we've raised small children, I've gotten used to distractions. I like music while I'm painting and will usually stop to answer the phone. If I just mixed some paint and don't want it to dry on my palette everyone can wait five minutes, until I finish that area, for their Kool-Aid. Because of

"Outlaw Justice" was a painting for the cover of a motorcycle novel written by my friend 'Bandit.' Check out his web-site at Bikernet.com.

working in this kid friendly environment I can now paint on location at Sturgis in front of 500,000 bikers. As I tell people, my kids have more horsepower than all those bikers combined. I often wake early in the morning and begin to paint as early as two or three o'clock. I can get in five or six hours painting time before anyone is awake. I can paint in all different frames of mind but never when I'm drinking. I just can't pay attention long enough or concentrate on what needs to get done. I can paint anytime, anywhere, using whatever I can for an easel, and getting by with just about any lighting. What is important to me and where I spend my money is on my brushes.

MY BRUSHES

There is just something about a cheap brush I can't stand. I guess it's like the master mechanic where a quality tool just feels better in his hand. You will get certain brushes and use them to death until all the hairs are falling out and you still don't want to part with them. I've always preferred natural hair brushes and not synthetic fibers. Acrylic paints will attack natural hair brushes and if not kept clean will only last for a short period of time. I'm told the synthetic fibers are much more durable, but I've never been able to paint with them. I don't care for the way synthetic brushes flex or carry paint. I'm a brush snob. Give me a Windsor Newton red sable, made in England, anytime. When I'm at the art store buying paint and brushes for a new project I don't even care about price.

Tools of the trade. An easel, lights, brushes, and paint – man, it just makes me want to get to work.

My all important brushes. My mechanic friends laugh at me because my tool box is so unorganized. Not so when it comes to my painting tools. Just like wrenches, there's a brush for every application.

While I buy brushes whenever I start a new painting I find it difficult to throw the old ones away. I've been stapling some of them to the back of original paintings so they can stay with the painting.

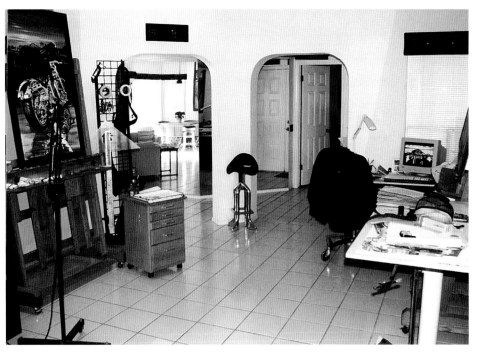

This studio space is in the dining room area of our home and has worked well for many years. I have two easels, a drawing table, desk, and computers. I'm currently building a new studio, and looking forward to it, but I doubt my art will be any better or worse because of it.

It's one of the few times I'm not price conscious. I may spend five or six hundred dollars on brushes and paint for a new work but if that painting sells for forty grand then it's money well spent. When I'm working I make sure the water jar I keep my brushes in is tall enough so just the tip of the brush handle sticks out. If you have more water in a vertical dimension, your brush will tend to float more and will not be lying on the bottom, bending the tip. When I'm finished for the day I take care to wash my brushes using dish soap and thoroughly rinse them. Make sure you get the dried paint out of the ferrule of the brush. It's the end up near the metal where all the hairs are connected. If paint is allowed to dry here the hairs will crack and fall out leaving you with an expensive toothpick. I use all styles of brushes to create different techniques. Rounds, Flats, Liners, Bristles, this will develop with time. I used to use only several styles of brushes but now have expanded as my paintings have developed. I use more colors on my palette, a larger selection of brushes, and have more sophisticated textures within my paintings because of it.

MY PALETTE

This is a tool I picked up in college. It's an enamel meat cutters tray. They can be found at most art stores. When they're not available or I need several palettes I will use a dinner plate. Never use a paper or Styrofoam plate. As I use acrylic paints, and they come in a gel form, you need to mix water with them to the correct consistency before you can paint. I've found the best surface for getting the correct consistency of your paint is a porcelain or enameled surface. Acrylic paints dry fast and paint will be wasted if it dries on your palette. The meat cutters tray can be placed in the refrigerator with your paints on it and will cool down keeping your paints workable for hours, or even days, if they are covered. When putting my paints on my palette I always start with the white and black in the same corner area as they are used more than the other colors. I then lay out my paints in groups of color: blues, reds, greens, as I move around the corner of the palette.

Keep the dark colors away from each other as they will get confusing. When put on your palette, before water is added, black, dark purple, and other colors

Placing the paints in a sequence on your pallet will save you a lot of frustration over time. It's easier to grab something when you know just where it's at.

When mixing paints, work in small amounts at a time until the correct color is achieved. When you get to that color you can always go back and mix larger amounts.

My paints of choice, Liquitex Acrylics. Different colors have varying densities: opaque, transparent, and translucent.

The base of my easel becomes a place for frequently used objects like paints, rulers, pencils, china markers, erasers, and a lupe (magnifying glass).

will all look the same. You'll be mixing colors and grab some of the wrong color and it will screw you up. You'll have to clean your brush and start all over to achieve the color mix you desire.

PAINTS

I paint with acrylic paints, all with a brush, no air brush or other mechanical medium. Always have, always will. There are a lot of ways to achieve any given solution but this system works for me. I only use Liquitex brand acrylic paints because I am familiar with their flow, colors, and characteristics. I have tried other brands when a particular color is out of stock, and while they work, I prefer Liquitex. They come in a gel form in a tube, and pre-mixed with water in jars. I use the tubes. Acrylic paints are said to be hard to work with because they dry fast and you can't blend colors. Not so if you learn about colors and how to mix them. Acrylics are suited to my style of painting, and my style may have developed because of the characteristics of this paint. They are bright, intense, exact, and can be manipulated to many different levels. I believe I can work with these paints for a lifetime and still will not have discovered all of their capabilities and limitations.

Acrylics can be used to create soft or hard edges and those hard edge lines I find desirable in painting mechanical objects like motorcycles. Because they dry fast, one color can be laid down next to another without a long waiting time. I can paint on location and pack things away easily without smearing a work in progress. They are a new generation of paint and they don't smell like oil paints. The only tools I need to work with are my palette, paints, brushes, and some water. I took an old painting and wanted to check the color fastness of these acrylic paints. Living in Phoenix, Arizona we have some of the most intense sunlight in the world. I hung a painting outside our home, by the pool, facing the southwest sun for over eight years. I could not detect any noticeable change in the colors of these paints over that period of time. I'm starting to sound like a salesman for Liquitex acrylic paints, but they are one of my tools of choice. At times I think maybe I'll try some oil paints, but why, when I'm still exploring the possibilities of this medium. Over the years I've worked with and have become very proficient with all the tools of the trade. Pen, pencil, charcoal, oils, and, I'm accomplished with them all. I've found that as your art capabilities develop the pinnacle has to be painting. It's like writing a novel compared to short stories. You are now at the top, working in full color, with the hardest paint in the world to master. You will spend the rest of your life exploring and trying to figure it out.

"Wicked" was a painting of top fuel drag racer Bill Furr at Sturgis one year. While there wasn't much detail in the bike I kept adding to the image and ended up hiding wicked images within the smoke.

Chapter Three

Establishing The Feeling

Your Personality in Paint

It is extremely important to establish a painting style. Colors and composition that will make your work different or recognizable from other artists. Expanding on that recognizable style, I try to mix up the composition or focus of my paintings while maintaining my style. For example: a close up view of a fuel tank, as in "Wash Day," or a full scenic view as in "Sturgis III." By mixing up the focus of each painting I don't get bored or repeat procedures. First I'll do a close up, next a painting with a human figure, then a complete, bike-only piece. I've found this

"Wash Day" was a major accomplishment for me. The original painting took over four months of painting nothing but bubbles. Very tedious, but the end result was worth the effort.

has made me a better artist as I get to practice on all textures and backgrounds. I've become equally capable of painting a human figure or a chrome exhaust pipe. To me there is nothing worse than an artist who paints a quality painting of a bike or car and then adds a human figure when they are not capable of painting one. It's just as important to have all the proportions of a figures hands and feet correct as it is as having the right amount of spring coils on a springer front end. Mixing up the focus of your paintings will make you a more well versed artist.

THE GRAPHIC OR CLOSE UP

I'll focus on two works to illustrate my thoughts as the process for these two paintings was similar. "Wash Day" and "The King of Flames." In "Wash Day" I had the initial idea of soap bubbles on a tank when I was washing my black motorcycle. I realized black wouldn't be the best color, so I hunted down a specific color and style of motorcycle. Props were put in to place, like the soap bubbles, and photographs were taken. In "The King of Flames," I was at a gas station during Laughlin and I was just staring at the reflection in the head light nacelle of the Road King that was next in line. Photographs were taken. Both of these initial painting reference photographs were similar. The initial photographs were taken with the composition and focus established before the painting was even started. The technique with which they were rendered made the style look like mine.

I staged the photo I used for "Wash Day" by finding the tank I wanted to use and talking the owner into letting me soap it up and shoot some pictures.

27

The original photo for the "King of Flames" as taken at a gas station while I was fueling up during the Laughlin River Run.

While I noticed the "Graphic Appeal" of these two works when I was photographing them, I intentionally tried to enhance specific elements while painting. I used several coats of the perfect red on "Wash Day" to achieve the richest red possible. The bubbles were created by analyzing them through a magnifying glass and then figuring out how to paint them. Likewise with "The King of Flames," where I analyzed the chrome through a magnifying glass to establish my hidden flames within the painting. Once I established specific elements, flames and bubbles, figured out how to render them, I then repeated those elements in a

During the painting of "The King of Flames" I decided to add flames within the work. My boys and I counted and estimated over 4000 flames were added to the image while keeping the integrity of the original photo.

graphic composition. What I feel this creates is a painting within a painting. Your view of either work from a distance is similar, they are bold and powerful. For some reason you are drawn in and want to look at these paintings closer. It's the intricacy and repeated patterns of the bubbles and flames that sucks you in. While this process can be boring and repetitious, the end result is worth it. I estimate well over 30,000 bubbles in "Wash Day" and over 4000 hidden flames in "The King of Flames." Both of these works were very time consuming with the painting time on each in excess of four months. There wasn't as much time spent on research or compiling reference photos but it was spent in the painting process. "Wash Day" was the first painting I ever sold before it was completed. While at Bike Week in Daytona 1994 a customer offered me $11,000. This work has been owned by several collectors, has been displayed in numerous museums, and is currently on the market for $54,000. The tedious task of painting all those buckin fubbles has long since been forgotten.

"The King of Flames" has also been a good, consistent, selling print, while the original also gathered a tidy sum. I enjoy long projects as the reward, both financial and artistically, is usually greater. I would not, however, like to do only close-up, graphic oriented works. I believe the

Over the years I've met a lot of interesting people. Bob Mills is a wildlife photographer who loaned me several photos he took in Alaska for my painting "Sturgis III." He took these in the wild from a distance of 400 yards.

mix of projects keeps an artist well versed and from falling into a rut of paintings that all look the same.

SCENIC VIEWS

Examined in this group of paintings are "Malibu," "Sturgis III," "Laughlin" and "Spikes Garage." All are paintings of entire bikes, set with scenery in the background. Some have figures, all with landscape, each recognizable as my style. While they all vary in subject matter, they all have certain similar characteristics. When painting a bike within a setting I try to give the

bike at least 40% of the overall canvas area. I believe if you get the bike too small you lose the feel of the work being a motorcycle painting. With that in mind I strive to create backgrounds that work with the motorcycle chosen. Be careful when creating a scenic painting to not make the background overpower the motorcycle.

I'm approaching losing the bike on "Spikes Garage" because the background has gotten so detailed and colorful. On "Malibu" I achieved the perfect harmony of bike and background

"Sturgis III" is a painting where I wanted to tell a story and capture a moment in time, just before it hits the fan. This is the same bear as in the previous photo standing up when he realizes someone is in his space.

that enhances the lines of that elegant FXR. The red bagger in "Sturgis" was chosen to work with the selected background. If I would have placed a black bagger in the same setting the painting would have been too dark and bland. The purple sky and ground in "Laughlin" are what makes that painting. Picture that piece with the background painted realistically. Black or dark grey pavement, dark green or sandy desert, a dark evening sky? The painting would not have been nearly as effective. Funny thing about the first "Laughlin" painting was I never thought it

The original photos taken of Coni for "Spikes Garage" were shot in a paint booth in Wisconsin two days before Christmas in a balmy 16 degree heat wave.

Two weeks after the Wisconsin heat wave I was out riding in the desert getting more reference material to complete the painting.

The mood for the entire Laughlin painting was established by my selection of colors.

would sell as well as it does. While I like the colors, the magentas and purples are some of my favorites to paint with, I thought the finished painting would look too feminine for a motorcycle painting. Just shows how much I know. The original painting sold immediately and the prints will be one of the first editions I have ever sold out of.

Painting scenic views are dramatically different than the close-up graphic views. A balance must be struck between motorcycle and background. The backgrounds generally are painted a lot looser than the bike and materialize faster. I usually just rough in the colors of the background before moving to the bike. When the

Photos for the painting "Malibu" were taken on the balcony of a mansion overlooking the ocean. We had to roll up Persian rugs and ride the bike through the home to get it out on the balcony.

bike is near completion I then go back and finish the background. Color choices and composition become increasingly more important. Both these skills come with time and practice. Painting a scene after a graphic is a welcome change as it is much looser and seems to come to life faster. Variety is the spice of life.

Interesting photos for "Spikes Garage" taken in Nothing, Arizona. Look at the beauty in the old rusted out car full of bullet holes.

This FXR was an incredibly classy machine and needed the correct background to enhance the subtle details of this bike. We spent half the day positioning the bike and waiting for the correct sunlight to shoot reference photos.

A selection of my prints on display during Daytona Bike Week. I've found it easier to post the prices (un-framed) than to constantly answer questions.

Chapter Four

Prints

My Thoughts on Reproduction of Artwork

Prints, or reproductions of original artwork, are often misunderstood and the whole concept is in need of some clarification. They are expensive, risky, and potentially rewarding to an artist's career. There are a number of printing methods available for reproducing original artwork, some have been around for hundreds of years, and others are new computer technologies. Most of them begin with photographic processes and I'll explain how mine are achieved.

An original on display in my exhibit. I keep in contact with my paintings and collectors. This one is on loan from Dan Bishop.

PHOTOGRAPHY

After completing an original painting I have them professionally photographed in a large format. The large format means that the film negatives used are either 4 x 5 inch or 8 x 10 inch. The larger the film negative, the better the clarity of the image when it is enlarged. I've found the 4 x 5 size works for me. The film captures plenty of detail and there plenty of photographers to chose from with the correct equipment and knowledge who are capable of shooting 4x5s. Find the best photographer available in your area that specializes in this type of work. Don't use someone who says, "I think I can do that." Your reproductions will only appear as good as the quality of your photographic reproductions. Professional photographers who shoot artwork and products will have the correct lighting and color balance to reproduce your

A stat camera used for photographing artwork for the Giclee' printing process.

artwork correctly. Expect to spend several hundred dollars on photographing each original. When I complete a painting I will have up to ten 4x5's and fifty 35mm slides reproduced of each image. Working from these transparencies, as they are called, you can have any type of prints created. I keep the original 4x5's of all my paintings in a fireproof safe. This is the photographic record of your artwork that you will need for a lifetime.

LITHO'S OR LITHOGRAPHS

These are the standard of the industry and how most printing is achieved these days. From business cards to catalogs to artwork the process remains the same. Different size equipment is used and different printers have their own specialties, but the process is the same. The principal of this process is that oil and water don't mix. Printing plates are created using the 4x5 transparency with some areas of the plate being receptive to oil (the printing ink) and others not. The advantage to Lithographs is they are cost effective when produced in large volumes.

They are of an extremely high quality and several commercial printers can be found in any good size town, capable of reproducing your artwork. The downside for an artist is that you will have to inventory the whole print edition, (in my case at least 1000 of each image), and shell out thousands of dollars, in advance, to create your prints. You have to be confident enough in your artwork and marketing abilities that you will recoup your initial printing investment. There are decisions to be made about paper, inks, and color correcting. The entire process of reproducing a painting to a lithographic print is costly, time consuming, and very exciting. When I am at the printing plant color correcting a print as it comes off the press and I know my ass is on the line, it's as exciting as completing a painting. Will these prints be a big seller? Did I just throw away thousands of dollars on 800# of paper that will sit in a warehouse? Over the years I have gotten to know what paper to use, what inks, and what printers are best suited to my work. I don't spare any expense at this point and use only the highest quality. My prints are reproduced on 80# or 100#, acid- free, pH balanced paper, using fade-resistant inks. They are stored in a climate-controlled warehouse to prevent moisture, mildew, or warping. Most of my images are reproduced as lithographic prints.

SERIGRAPHS

A serigraph is a fancy name for a screen print. The art community is good at coming up with names that make artwork sound more expensive. One usually thinks of a screen print as a t-shirt but a serigraph as art. Same thing. The process involves pushing the ink through a stencil or screen. The advantage is large amounts of ink can be applied to the paper making the artwork very brilliant. Serigraphs are often done by hand and don't require mechanical presses, making them costly and time consuming. Another advantage is they can be created in very large formats using screens as large as rooms. A correctly done serigraph is colorful and an art form in its own right. I haven't reproduced any of my motorcycle paintings as fine art serigraphs and it seems they are becoming less common with the advent of new computer printing processes.

GICLEE'

Pronounced Gee-Clay. When they first came out several years ago I was calling them guy-slees. "Give me a couple of them there guy-slees." It's just another fancy name for an ink jet print. It's actually a French word meaning spurts of ink. An interesting note here is that Graham Nash of *Crosby, Stills, Nash, and Young* fame was one of the founders and financial concerns backers behind the development of this new technology. Original artwork from your 4x5 transparency is scanned into a computer, digitized, color corrected, and then output on a large format ink jet printer. The advantage to the artist is the prints can be reproduced one at a time without the thousands of dollars in cash outlay. They can also be adjusted for color with each printing. Giclee's can be printed on a number of different surfaces including canvas. As it is relatively new technology they are constantly getting better as both as an art form and a means of reproduction. The downside is that the unit cost of Giclee's remains very high, driving up the individual print price. There are also a number

of Giclee' printers popping up and very few are capable of producing a quality reproduction. I've gone through several printers (paying set-up fees each time) that have gone under, or couldn't maintain my quality standards. I believe this method of printing will only get better over the years, but has a way to go before it catches up to the lithographic technology.

LIMITED EDITION PRINTS

Limited Edition Prints means exactly what it says. To limit the edition or amount of prints produced. Most of my print editions are 950. They are signed and numbered meaning each print is individually inspected by me for quality and, color… before I sign it. They will then be numbered like 2/950. This will mean that print is the second print available in a total allotment of 950 prints. The lower number prints are usually con-

This is the cleanest automatic screen printing press I've ever seen. My friends at Paramount Screen Print do a meticulous job on my t-shirts.

sidered more valuable. In an edition of 950 prints I save number 1 and number 950 for my two boys. It's kind of like an artist's 401K plan for when I'm gone. As a print gets closer to being sold out I usually increase the price. After all, when they're all sold out the only way you can get one is on the secondary market. This means buying one from someone who already owns one. I've recently doubled the price on two different prints when they reached number 800 of an edition of 950. When these prints get to number 900, I will double the price again for the last 50 prints. It's kind of like owning a home. If you like the house and the area you may never sell it. It's still nice to know that it's worth more than you paid for it. Your customers that initially bought a print will also get a better deal by buying in at an early date. I now have a number of repeat customers built up over the years and I've pre-sold as many as 100 prints before a new print edition is even released. This often allows me to pay for the entire print run and not have to be out of pocket with my cash. An open edition print can be of the same high quality as a limited edition print, but they

will not be numbered. They are generally signed by the artist but by not assigning numbers the artist can print as many as they like. Sometimes up to 50,000 or 75,000 copies. Open edition prints are not as costly or collectable as limited edition prints.

ARE THEY PRINTS OR POSTERS?

What is the difference between a print and a poster? This gets very confusing to people who haven't collected art. A poster usually has some graphics or type associated with the image. A black border or the title of the work in large letters may border the art. Posters are of lesser quality than prints. Normally not on a heavy paper, and not printed with the same quality of ink. They can be signed but are usually not numbered. These differences account for the greater cost of a print.

ARTIST PROOFS

Artist proofs or A/P's as they are called, are an often-misunderstood item. When I am first printing an image I always go to the printer for what is called a press check. When the prints are first being run I will be there at the final stage of quality control to check the colors, size, quality of printing… as the prints are first being produced. In any given print run the size or edition should be designated. For example, 950 limited edition prints, 50 artist proofs. A total of 1000 prints of this size and format are originally being produced. The artist proofs are the first prints off of the press that I have inspected. They may vary slightly in color as adjustments are made, but for the most part resemble the additional print run of 950 prints. After color corrections are made and the A/P's are printed, I leave and the

A smaller screen printing press. These presses are sized by the amount of colors they can print. Some of my art is reproduced on t-shirts in up to eighteen colors.

printer will complete his job referring back to the A/P's to make sure the quality is consistent. Artist Proofs usually cost more and are more collectable. As there are not as many A/P's as there are limited editions, collectors usually prefer A/P's. For the most part A/P's are of the same quality as the rest of the print run. Over the years I have seen all kinds of designations assigned to prints. Publishers proofs, printers proofs, etc.... While I'm not really sure what all these designations mean, I believe it's a money thing and personally would avoid everything except A/P's. Some artists number their A/P's, I prefer not to. My reason is that many of my A/P's are given out to preferred customers, celebrities, and people within the motorcycle industry. I don't want to hear people saying that they have A/P number one, what number do you have? It's just one less thing to worry about.

CANVAS PRINTS

Canvas prints are exactly that, prints on canvas. They can be created several different ways and are, for the most part, new technology. The best of these canvas prints are Giclee' prints on canvas. The same printing process is used, only applied to canvas instead of paper. I re-touch my Giclee' canvas prints, meaning I personally go back and paint on top of the print, adding some highlights and giving each print a unique look. Some artists have assistants that go back and retouch their prints. When these prints first became available I was opposed to them. Being old school, I was of the attitude that there should only be one image on canvas and that should be the original painting. I thought that these prints would kind of slight the owner of the original painting that paid the big bucks. I have changed my mind for several reasons. My original paintings are large in scale and

One of my displays during a motorcycle event. Sometimes I'm in an art gallery, sometimes a rubber tent on an asphalt parking lot. Not always glamorous, always exciting.

the Giclee' canvas prints are much smaller. While the quality of these prints has gotten so good I would hope no one mistakes them for an original. They are not originals. Even though re-touched, they are prints.

Canvas artwork does not need to be protected by glass as paper prints do. They frame up easier and view much better. After you have achieved the level of collecting canvas prints, I doubt you will go back to paper prints. By re-touching each print they all become individual. I originally thought this re-touching process would be boring but I actually enjoy it. After working on the original painting for several months you may get to a point where the art is looking so good you don't want to take any chances. Should I add some purple to the sky? No I better not screw it up. So now you are re-touching these canvas Giclee's and you can take all those liberties you didn't want to try on the

original work of art. Care must be taken when producing the canvas Giclee's because of the current inks being used. All the inks are water based and unless properly top coated will blur and rinse off if they get wet. Make sure you have a good printer with the correct method of top coating or you will end up with some really pissed off customers. Imagine a customer paying $2500 for a canvas Giclee' and bragging to his friends how he met the artist at Sturgis. He then goes to wipe down the artwork that has gotten dusty over the last several months, and the image wipes off with a paper towel. Not cool. Unless it's been properly top coated. You also can not re-touch the canvas prints using water-based paints, unlike the acrylic paints I prefer to use. Canvas prints also fall in the price range between paper prints and the original painting. This gives your customers another cost and quality option. I also like to use these prints

My assistant Lisa explains the details of a painting to customers. Getting out there and showing your art is an absolute necessity.

40

to display my artwork at shows. As most of my originals are sold, or are large and hard to transport, these canvas Giclees' are a good alternative.

T-SHIRTS

T-shirts are deserving of some attention but there are some challenges associated with them. I've owned several T-shirt screen printing businesses and have printed millions of t-shirts. To an artist all they will offer you is some promotional value and spread your name out more. I highly doubt that your images on a t-shirt will get you rich. If they do it's because your artwork and name have already risen to that level and now everyone wants your t-shirt. They are a problem to print, inventory, and sell. Make sure you understand what you are taking on or you will end up giving out a lot of free t-shirts for Christmas. For exam

-ple, you decide to take ten of your favorite paintings and produce them on t-shirts. They come in four different sizes. You now have forty part numbers to inventory and distribute. Change the color of shirt from white to black and you have eighty part numbers to inventory. The t-shirt industry is just that, an industry. It is highly competitive and very price conscious. If you decide to print t-shirts approach it with the promotional value in mind, not with the idea of making money. The number of T-shirt lines that have become successful are few and far between compared to the number of failures. If it sounds like I'm disenchanted with t-shirts, I am not. They are just very time consuming and much more challenging than they would initially appear. Time spent on t-shirts could be devoted to creating more artwork.

A selection of my art shows a number of different types of reproductions. Screen prints for the t-shirts, lithos on the framed prints, and a large canvas Giclee' print of "Wired."

"Daytona" is a colorful study of chrome. A very large painting measuring almost six feet tall, it is in the collection of Mike Corbin, motorcycle saddle maker.

Chapter Five

Chrome Sweet Chrome

Painting a Reflection

Fascinating isn't it? How do you paint chrome? Do you use chrome paint? These are some of the most frequently asked questions. By now you should understand that I'm in the observation business. When I look at a group of clouds, or a sunset, I analyze the colors and figure out how I'd paint them. Chrome takes a lot of observation and the understanding that it is only the reflection of its surroundings. If you look at the sky and can't figure out how to paint it, or don't see the different hues of blue going from blue green to a purple blue, then you will never be able to figure out how to paint chrome as it picks up the reflection of the sky. I may be able to give you a few pointers, but observation and understanding where the reflections are coming from is the key to chrome.

"Dangerous," "Casino," "Billet Proof" and "The King of Flames" are all examples of chrome paintings. Each unique, but the painting principals are the same. In "Billet Proof" I wanted a softer image. The challenge was to create a painting of a motor - a subject usually perceived as a dirty mechanical object - and make it soft enough to hang on a living room wall. The reflections in the chrome were toned down and the edges were softened. The exhaust pipes in "Billet Proof" were rendered in a different way than the hard edges of the reflections in "The King of Flames." Both appear as chrome. "Dangerous" was created specifically to demon-

strate my ability to paint chrome. The reflections are recognizable and exact. "Casino" is not usually recognized as a painting of chrome but

The reference photo for "Daytona" was a quickie photo taken at a bike show as I was walking through. Part of the character of this photo comes from all of the lighting from the indoor convention center.

"Casino" was based upon a Ron Simms built bike which was purchased by Jason Giambi (baseball star). The bike is a beautiful example of polished aluminum and chrome.

was actually one of the harder chrome works I've ever done. The bike, built by Ron Simms and owned by Jason Giambi (baseball star) was a masterful work of chrome and polished aluminum. There was chrome reflecting off of chrome. Very challenging. In addition to the motor I had the springer front end to contend with. When you think you have chrome mastered, paint a springer.

EXHAUST PIPES

I'll use these as an example because they're curved and appear on most motorcycles. The principals discussed here will apply to various parts of chrome, especially curved surfaces. Take a look at a pipe that runs horizontally, photograph it, and study it through a magnifying glass. Turn around and take a picture of the surroundings. You'll be using the same colors. Chances are that the top of the pipes show as blue. They are a compressed view of the sky. The sky colors will change from a blue purple directly overhead, to a blue green at a 45% angle in front of you, to a washed out white blue directly in front of you. If you live in Chicago where I grew up, they will be varying shades of grey. In Arizona, you will have beautiful blues. These colors will be used for the top 50% of our imaginary horizontal exhaust pipe. There will then appear a darker line, it's the horizon line or buildings reflected behind you. This will be the portion of the pipe that is closest to you in the paint-

The original "Casino" photo was taken in passing at a bike show in L.A. It took a lot of studying to break the chrome down to workable elements.

The original photo taken for "Billet Proof" was from an early bike built by Paul Yaffe. I added in the turquoise color in the painting as I felt it worked well with Paul's original color scheme on the bike.

"Billet Proof" was intentionally treated to a softer effect on the chrome than the hard edge style of "Casino". The original painting hangs in the mansion where the "Malibu" bike was photographed, next to an original Picasso.

ing. Our pipe will then start to bend away from you until it vanishes and begins to turn away like the dark side of the moon. The bottom 50% of our pipe will be composed of the ground colors, going from the distance below our horizon line to the closest terrain to the pipes. If your bike is parked on gravel or grass you will be able to see specific blades of grass or pebbles of gravel reflected near the bottom of the pipe. These details will diminish and become blurred or unrecognizable as they head towards the horizon line on our pipes. A trick I use here is to immediately paint the horizon line on the pipes using a color made up of both background colors. If I have a blue sky and a brown rock ground, I will mix the blue and the brown to create a dark blue brown which is the color I will use for my horizon line. Please bear in mind this is a basic chrome formula. If you have a red building behind you, that will appear above the horizon line. The bottom line is you have to notice the reflections and create a painting within a painting. Very time consuming. Painting chrome will take a lot of

patience to do correctly. When I'm painting intricate areas of chrome rendering a polished motor or billet wheel I may get four square inches done in an eight hour period.

The horizontal exhaust pipes are good practice and an easy place to start. It gets more com-

A close up of "Dangerous" shows me riding my Jesse James built bagger in the background. At the time of this painting there were very few flamed baggers and the painting has only added to the notoriety of the bike.

plex from there. The pipes will bend upward and start to pick up reflections from the color of the frame or the bottom of the tank. The same curved principals applied on the pipes will also be used on the bike's rims, only in reverse. The blues of the sky are the bottom of the rim, while the brown rocks will be on the top of the rim. Look at the angle that each area of chrome is facing and think about what would appear 180-degrees in front of that surface. The bottom of the fender struts will pick up the ground, the top of the struts the sky color, and the flat sides may pick up a combination of both, or just one, depending upon the angle of the bike on the kickstand. Painting chrome is both fascinating and challenging. There is an important balance

that needs to be kept. Chrome appears fluid because you are not usually standing completely still when viewing an object. If you render it too exactly it tends to lose any motion. You must decide on the balance of your chrome. You can make it fluid, stagnant or somewhere in between. I try not to vary my chrome techniques within the same painting. If I'm painting the chrome on "Billet Proof" soft, then I'll carry that "soft" technique throughout the painting. Hard edge chrome as in "The King of Flames" carried a different technique throughout. The colors used, and technique of painting chrome varies from painting to painting, the concept of how to paint it should be kept consistent. Think of it as another surface texture, just like water or

A close up of "Malibu" shows the subtle changes in the chrome that make the bike look realistic. The bluing of the exhaust pipes adds to the credibility that this is a real, ridden, motorcycle.

rubber or leather, but start to create a painting within a painting. If you can look at a cloud and start to see other objects then you can figure out chrome. You're in the observation business.

A close up of "Shovelheat" shows how the reflections change from the ground to the sky. Find the skulls on the pushrod tubes?

Close up details on "Not Pork" show the reflections of the sky as well as the grass. The browns picked up in the chrome are from the leaves lying on the ground.

Chapter Six

Wired

A Step-by-Step Sequence

"Wired" was a commissioned painting for a new customer I met during Bike Week in Daytona Beach Florida. By a commissioned work, I mean a painting done specifically for that individual. I try not to do too many commissioned paintings, as I have more of my own ideas than I have time to paint. There are exceptions though, like when you get a call from the

"Wired" turned out to be a dramatic balance of color and composition. The angles and lines of the bike have been enhanced by the choice of background elements.

Indianapolis Motor Speedway. This was one of those exceptions.

Steve approached me at my booth and asked if I'd like to do a painting of his bike. I told him I don't normally do commissioned paintings and tried to politely turn him down. About an hour or so later he pulled up on his bike, a very nicely done chopper built by Eddie Trotta, a well known bike builder. After talking for a while, Steve and I came to an agreement that I could use any background, change anything I deemed necessary - and basically do whatever I chose. Steve was also only purchasing the painting - I retained all copyrights. This meant I could use the image for t-shirts or limited edition prints at a later date.

I lined up a time where I could photograph the bike before I bailed out of Bike Week. Steve showed up at a location on the beach early in the morning when I thought the light would be good for my photos. While I'm an amateur photographer at best, I try to take my own reference photos. They may not be the best photos but I'm looking for certain angles and details of the bike that are important to me. As I use these photos only for reference the colors and background may, and probably will, change by the time the painting is completed. We found an area that has a boardwalk and rode the chopper out on it. Over about an hour's time, I moved the bike, lay on the ground, and basically climbed all over to get the angles I thought would work. All of this time I'm pondering the design elements of the bike and composition of the painting. I feel this layout of the painting, and the bike, in my mind

The original "Wired" photograph has the basics for a great painting but lacks the dramatic colors and contrast created in the painting.

A study of razor wire shows there is a lot more to painting it than one would initially imagine. Even though I've altered the colors in the painting these 'photo studies' are helpful in rendering any image.

is one of the most important steps in creating a great work. You can have a great bike for subject matter and be skilled with your paints at rendering, but if you don't understand or have a feel for design and layout your paintings will fall short of their full potential. Photos, lots of photos, were taken from all angles.

Analyzing the lines of this particular bike I found the strongest elements to be the long lines created by the front end and the perpendicular line of the frame shooting toward the back tire. I also liked the size and strength of the back tire and wanted that in the foreground. The wood in the boardwalk was also positioned so the boards drew your attention toward the motor. All of this composition needed to be done in advance in my mind to create eye movement. This design sense and ability to create eye movement within a painting is something I attribute to my schooling and years of creating art. It's something that I am always thinking about, but mostly on an unconscious level. You'll know when it's right, because you can feel it.

Back in my studio, with all my photos laid out on my drawing table, I begin a selection process to choose the best angles from

The penciled in image of "Wired" took several days to complete. Details like the razor wire were added later.

the photographs taken. After I have selected several I examine them through a loupe, which is a printer's magnifying glass. I'll check for the focus and clarity of the photos I've selected. Once I've made my decision, I'll bring the negatives to a photo lab and have them enlarged to 10x12 inches or larger. This will make everything easier to see and also easier to draw. With all my reference photos ready to go I'm about ready to begin the painting. I'm already in this project a month at this point. The next step is to get your image drawn upon the canvas. There's a saying that your first four lines are the ones defined by the edge of your canvas. Keeping this in mind I determine the size of my canvas and how large the bike will be within that space. I assemble and stretch my own canvas. The size of the canvas is determined by the image. Don't try to fit an image on to a canvas that is pre-made or is not the correct size. In the back of my mind I've determined how much sky I want and other elements like the barbed wire that will be added later. With all of that considered I'm ready to start drawing the bike at the size and angle that have been selected.

Armed with my blank white canvas, reference photos everywhere, pencils (2B & 4H), erasers, and a spray workable fixative I start drawing. Using the 4H pencil, the lighter of the two, I sketch out my subject once again beginning with the strong visual elements. The long lines of the frame, front end, and the massive back tire are the start of this drawing. My method of drawing is to work from the outside in. Establish shapes and move in towards the details. Use the lighter

Paint is being laid on to establish the background colors and what colors I will eventually use in the chrome.

4H pencil and when you're comfortable with a certain area use the darker 2B pencil. I'll then erase the lighter sketch lines of the 4H pencil leaving the distinct lines of the 2B. The fixative is a spray barrier that goes between the pencil lines and your hand and the paints. Spray small areas at a time as you work up the drawing and you'll keep your drawing clean and accurate. Time spent on your drawing will save you weeks later in the painting stages. There are many ways of getting your image onto the canvas. I prefer to draw mine because that is something I enjoy and also feel I excel at. Some artists draw grids on the canvas and reference photos and break the drawing down to small sections. Other photo-realist artists may even use slides and project the image on the canvas. These days computer generated images can be scanned and printed on canvas. I'm an artist and I like to draw. Take however long it takes to complete a drawing with which you are comfortable. With both the painting and the drawing I need that time to look at my finished work, usually at the end of the day, taking notes on what I want to change, fix, or edit. This drawing process will take me no less than two days. When completed, I'll have a neat, accurate drawing that I will spray with the fixative for a protective coating.

THE PAINTING PROCESS

All of my paintings are done only with a brush using acrylic paints. I draw and paint with my hands, rarely using mechanical tools such as an airbrush or other means. This is my technique, and my tools and paints of choice. As with any

As I work up the colors in the painting you can see all of the blues and purples that have been used in the wood. While these colors may not be immediately noticeable, they will tie the background colors in with the woodwork.

project the end result can be accomplished in many ways. I'll explain how I do it. I normally start with black paint, straight from the tube, and begin to block in the large dark areas of the bike and background. Look for negative spaces, areas where there is not much detail. Dark areas in the motor, spaces between the wheels and frame, some of the tire outlines. This will accomplish several things, one of which is to examine the proportions of your drawing before you get too far into the painting process. Acrylics dry fast and can be painted on top of. There are a lot of dark areas on motorcycles, such as in the engine. I've found that I'll paint these areas entirely black and will go in later with a white pencil and draw the details on top of the black paint. Over the years I've found I use less black in the beginning of the

painting than I used to. In early paintings I used the black paint as I would my pencils, outlining areas and filling in between. While this works and you can always paint over the black outline, I've done enough paintings and have polished my technique to a point where I know what works for me and where I'm going with the painting.

When I have my blacks worked up to a comfortable point the next step is to establish the basis of colors I will be using in the painting. This next step in laying down colors is usually a quick process of laying down a thinned out transparent layer of color. You can paint over your drawing lines and still see them. These base colors are laid down for several reasons. Establish the mood of your painting by utilizing color. The original photos for "Wired" were taken during

At this point I'm beginning to work up my chrome colors on the headlight and front forks. I've also begun to shade the sheet metal of the bike to give it some dimension.

the day and looked very cute against the beach setting. It was my intention to make this painting a little more menacing, I chose a night setting darkening up the wood and background. Establishing these night colors would give me a direction to move in. Most of my motorcycle paintings have an abundance of chrome and polished parts. I'll get in to the specifics of painting chrome in another chapter, but the bottom line is, chrome reflects the colors of the surroundings. By establishing these base colors you will know what colors to use on your chrome. Just as in the photographs and the drawing, composition and eye movement within the painting are very important at this point in time. I've laid out the barbed wire and the grain of the wood to flow with the movement of the bike. Very subtle

painting and composition techniques that many people will not even notice but the overall effect will make a world class painting. Sometimes in a painting you will feel like you've gotten so deep no one but you will notice your efforts. Who cares? As long as you are happy with your accomplishments that's what matters.

I now have my background base colors, have established my mood, the blacks are in place, and I'm getting toward the specifics. The sheet metal is next and will also be an important color because it will be reflected in the chrome in numerous areas. I've found it valuable to think in terms of surface textures and group these elements. Example: Sheet metal, tires, wood, chrome, sky. They all have their own feel and each presents a certain challenge to paint. In

With the sheet metal painted and the flames added I'll move on to another area. Later I'll return and add highlights from a light source that will be consistent on the chrome and the sheet metal.

56

painting the sheet metal I want to achieve that shiny metal finish which differs greatly from the porous rubber tires. Look through the graphics of the paint job and analyze the flow of the metal. Choose the colors you will use and notice where the brightest and darkest areas of the sheet metal lie. Notice that I've shaded the sheet metal using colors and haven't used any blacks or whites to create the curves of forms. The metal should flow at this point with no abrupt changes. Look for areas of reflected light, underneath the tank, along the bottom of the frame, or that one orange line that outlines the boundary between the tank and the wood. Continually go back to a reference point and monitor your colors. If you decided the brightest orange of the bike was on the top of the tank, then what color is the back

fender compared to the tank? I may throw some flames or graphics on the bike at this point, but it is only to establish colors I will use in the future. As I move inward toward the details of the painting I like to complete areas to about 80% of the finished product. Towards the end of the painting I will complete this last 20%, which I've found ties all of the elements of the finished painting together.

Moving from the sheet metal to the chrome once again, I need to establish a basis of colors for my chrome. I've found the rims and motor to be the most challenging areas of chrome to paint, so I'll begin establishing my colors on a relatively easy area such as the headlight. As I mentioned, chrome will reflect the colors of the surroundings. Analyzing the headlight I notice reflections from

Notice how blue the tires are at this point. These are the same blues used in the sky. By adding more color to the painting over the original photograph, I've increased the dramatic effect of the image.

the sky, the horizon and terrain behind the viewer, and the wood of the boardwalk. The challenge in this painting is that I am artificially creating background colors that differ greatly from the original photographs. As the chrome of the headlight picks up the night sky an observation of a sky is important. Most sky, colors are composed of several shades of blue. A cool blue or blue green was used in this sky as well as a warm blue, purple blue. Often the horizon line, as in this headlight, is composed of both the sky colors and the terrain colors. The line or horizon down the middle of the headlight is blue mixed with the red browns of the boardwalk. As I paint my chrome colors in, using colors from the background, I can move laterally in any direction as my background colors have just been roughed in.

Time is spent on the headlight, front fork tubes, and handlebars as the colors I use in these will be mimicked in the much harder areas of the motor and wheels. As in all my paintings I am not out to duplicate a photograph. I like to think I'm turning up the volume, brightening up my colors, and altering them as I see fit to create a mood that suits the individual painting. Now that I have my chrome colors established I move to other areas of the bike, concentrating on the chrome. Paint similar angles of reflections at the same time. Both pipes are on the same angle and therefore have similar reflections. Observe the angles of the metal and decide which pieces will be painted the blues of the sky, the browns of the boardwalk, and where orange will be reflected off of the frame. Chrome is very time consuming

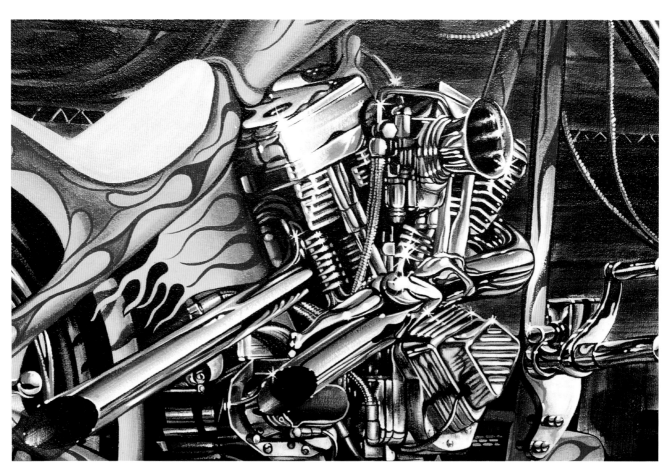

A close up reveals how colorful the chrome actually is. Notice the nude figure on the exhaust pipe. It's actually a small sculpture titled "Exhausted" that can be purchased. I love the humor.

and this painting took over a month to just complete the chrome work alone. There is also a difference between polished aluminum and chrome. The edges of colors on polished parts are not as sharp as they are on chrome. Notice the engine block and oil pump differ from the rocker boxes at the top of the motor. There is no way to rush this process, and you will only get out of a painting the effort you decide to put into it.

Sticking to my format of painting surface textures I've moved along to the tires. The back tire is predominant in this painting and is also the closest part of the motorcycle to the viewer. Objects that are closer to you have more color, contrast, and clarity than more distant objects. Notice the detail of the rear tire compared to the front. I decided the rear tire needed a lot of work

to make it jump off of the canvas. I mixed several different grays to create the back tire. Areas of the tire facing the sky were mixed with the blues of the sky. As the tire bends inward on the sides, browns of the boardwalk were mixed in. The shadows from the fender moving in and out of the tire become very important in creating depth. The rubber has a porous feel and a different brush is used so the tires remain distinct from other elements of the bike. Small pebbles have been added and stuck in the tires to add detail and character. While the front tire has the small pebbles the shading and colors are muted compared to the back tire.

With the bike 80% complete I move to the background, which was only roughed in earlier. Using a long straightedge I make the gaps

You can see the purples in the headlight and forks that are actually reflections of the wooden boardwalk. Don't overlook items like braided cables and make sure they are all there or someone will call you on it.

between the boards. These will be drawn in with a white grease pencil and painted in with black. There's a small gap in the boards behind the bike where the chain link fence will show through. Once again, drawn in white pencil, and then painted. The wood is worked up and becomes

darker while I start to give some more grain to the wood following the flowing lines of the bike. I'm careful at this point to not make the wood too detailed as it will compete and distract from the bike. I've made that mistake before. It's all about the bike. While the wood was only worked to a moderate degree, I had questions about the barbed wire and chain link fence. My initial thoughts were to make the razor wire chrome and mimic the colors in the bike, but I was concerned about focusing too much on the fence and not the bike. When in doubt, take some reference photos. Once again I was off to find some razor wire and a chain link fence for reference photos. I took some close ups and distant shots and then created my own version. The razor wire flows with the bike and creates eye movement and all the elements work together. Not as many colors were used on the fence as in the chrome of the bike so as not to compete. The fence is also behind the bike and therefore wouldn't have the colors and clarity of the chrome in the bike. Notice the bottom of the fence pole above the gas tank picks up an orange reflection from the bike's gas tank. Cool stuff.

A detail of the rear wheel shows the time spent in painting a tire. Certain areas have been painted solid black and I've gone back in with white 'China Marker' to draw my details. These areas will be painted on top of the black.

Completing the background are the shadows of

the bike on the boardwalk. These shadows are an area often overlooked and one of my personal pet peeves. If you didn't put the shadows under the bike and tires the bike would appear to be floating. You need to study shadows, rarely are they solid black. Usually a shadow is transparent and often a deep or dioxanine purple. Some shadows have a crisp edge; others are soft, depending upon how and where the light is falling on the subject.

Signing of a painting is always a highlight to me. One of my past jobs was as a sign painter and I take as much pride in signing my paintings as I do in painting them. Care is chosen in where to sign, what colors to use, and in keeping my signature consistent with other works. It also signals the completion of a three-month project.

When I sign my paintings, I've decided they are completed.

The finished piece will still be around for some time while I make sure all elements are complete. I check for pencil and grease pencil marks to be removed, and the painting is wiped down with a light soap and water to remove any foreign matter. When it's completely dry I'll spray the surface with one of several coatings available to protect from UV rays or enhance the shine. Often the large black areas of a painting will appear to have a dull finish and other areas will have a shine. These spray coatings balance out the overall finish. Now comes the hard part, a title, and what price will I put on it.

At this point "Wired" is 80% complete and I will now move around the canvas and start to tie all the areas together, not concentrating on any specific elements.

Chapter Seven

Dangerous

The All-Important Research

"Dangerous" is a classic example of how a concept and painting will evolve over time. For a number of years I've had this concept in my mind and finally got around to putting the components down on canvas. When you're riding up on one of those shiny tankers it's like riding past a mirrored window on a store front. It's a fleeting moment in time. You always glance over to check out you and

Who would have thought that a painting of a truck and some bikes would become so popular? That's the thing about true art. It can't be decided in a boardroom or by a committee. It should just be created and let the public decide.

your ride, but then the light turns green and you blast off. You never really get a good look at the mirrored image. One of my challenges was to freeze that moment in time so you could check out everything that's going on. In addition to that initial challenge, one of the most frequently asked questions is, "How do you paint chrome?" I wanted to take the opportunity on this painting to show people exactly how chrome is painted. With the large expanse of polished stainless on the trailer it would be easier to explain how I break down colors, than on a small area like exhaust pipes.

Back to the initial concept. I'd been talking to a few friends about this idea before I started, and as usual, some of them look at you like you're crazy. A few people get it, but I think most people can't visualize it until it's down on canvas. So I knew I had a strong idea because most bikers have experienced this situation, but only a select few could visualize it. There were several notable conversations about this work that I'll never forget. One was with a club member named Tiny at Laughlin years ago. Tiny was instrumental in getting David Mann's, (the original motorcycle artist) career started. Tiny and I talked about this work and how he had mentioned the concept to Dave several times and Dave never got

around to doing it. Well, as an artist you're always hearing you should do this or that and until the concept really strikes you, you just blow off that input. I guess Dave never got around to doing it, but I was always impressed with the imagination of his work. Just the knowledge that another artist, whose work I admire, had contemplated this idea,

Initial photos from the Jesse bagger are helping me to get perspectives and distortions in the rear of the tanker. Notice the lack of color in the sky and surroundings, and how all that will be brightened up in the painting.

got me even more intrigued. Another conversation was with Arlen Ness, the most famous and respected bike builder of all time. Arlen wanted a painting of mine for a new showroom he was building. We talked about this concept, and I was originally going to put Arlen on one of his choppers reflected in the back of the tanker. His son Cory was to be on the bike blasting by in the no passing zone. Arlen's in northern California and I'm in Arizona and a lot of reference photos were going to be needed for this work. We just never put it together. These were two of the visionaries that understood the painting before it was even started.

Now I've got the basis for an exciting new painting. Both the challenge and the fun of this painting were already proving to be in the

research. I was going to need photos, lots of photos. I'd been involved in the trucking industry for a good part of my life. Lining up the tanker only took half a dozen phone calls. I called Casey at Roads West. They're a west coast trucking company with a couple of hundred semis. I designed their logo when I was in college for $300 and they had only two trucks. Casey sent me to Beall trailers, and a phone call later I had a new stainless chemical tanker available only 20 miles away. I called a friend (I thought we might need two bikes and photographers for the initial reference photos) and we jumped on the bikes, loaded with film and cameras, and hooked it over to Beall Trailers. They were very accommodating and pulled the trailer to an empty lot jockeying the rig several times to get it in the correct lighting position. Being an artist

More photo angles were needed to get the bike distortions correct. I'm on the bagger and a buddy is shooting the pictures just to the left.

allows you access to situations like this. Act professional, hand them a catalog, explain who you are, what you're doing, and tell them you'll send them one of the first prints when the image is completed. Follow up on sending out the freebies for the people and companies that have helped you. Now Beall trailers has a low number on the "Dangerous" print and I'm sure it is hanging in a prominent place in their office. This is all great P.R. and makes you a person of your word, even though the prints were probably not ready for at least a year after this photo shoot. Thanks to Roads West & Beall.

So we've got the trailer, two bikes, and I'm ready to get the first photos for a painting idea. This is serious shit. I've been talking about this work, figuring it out in my mind, and it all begins

here. They may sell the trailer and I may never have this perfect set-up again. Remember, at this point, I've only got ideas floating around in my head. I don't know what angles I'm going to shoot. All of the elements you see in the painting, like the bike passing on the left, came later. If I had used photos shot from directly behind, the whole painting would be different. It was also at this point that both the title and a theme developed. Usually I don't title my paintings until they're finished. They change and evolve so much I've found titling them at the end works for me. I needed a placard for the back and asked the Beall dude what they had. He mentioned a few and then said "Dangerous." Perfect, I liked it. As this painting developed I stuck with the entire "Dangerous" theme, adding dangerous elements to the painting.

These angles helped me figure out how to paint the reflections of the forward mud guards on the tanker. By taking lots of photos, and studying them, you will understand the subject better.

65

Both the title and theme came about in a trucking company dirt lot. Cool.

Butch and I set to work getting some shots. Close ups of me on my bagger. Distance photos to get the perspective of the truck. Shots of how the sky interacted with the stainless of the trailer. I had some weird reflections in the trailer - like trucks parked in the background, but that's OK. I'd deal with that later and left knowing I'd taken some good reference photos. I bee-lined over to Walgreen's so I could get one hour developing. While only a dozen photos are shown in this book I shot 6 rolls of film on just the trailer. Back at the studio I laid them all out on my drawing table and started to select the angles and elements I was going to use. I came up with a good rear view I thought would work, and some close-ups of me on the Jesse Bagger. The rear view was enlarged to an 8 x 10, so that was my central focus to be used on this painting.

The background within the tanker had to be figured out. The reflections of the dirt lot had to be replaced with a road scene. This was going to be tough. No reference photos here, I had to do it from memory. One of the things I remembered from art school is that you have a very poor visual memory. So I analyzed my tanker photos and thought about what I needed. How the clouds would reflect when the truck was moving. Where would the horizon line appear on both the side of the truck and in the rear? This way when I ended up behind a tanker, I would consciously know what to look for. Well it was time for Hollister, I'd be taking a ride west until I hit the ocean and then right to Hollister. There are a lot of tankers running this route and I knew I'd run across a few. Everything in this painting just kind of fell into place. It took some time, but the end result was worth the wait. I pulled out of Phoenix and hit I-10 to L.A. where I was meeting Kenny from Samson Exhaust.

This view of the back of my bike is a friend John's favorite. Come to think of it, it's the only view he has ever seen of my bike.

Outside of Phoenix I pulled up behind a shiny Benito tanker. This company has the cleanest tankers on the road. I followed this driver for over an hour. Pulling in close, 3 or 4 feet away, dropping back, weaving from side to side. I had the opportunity to check out all the reflective items I needed. All I had to do was remember them. I thought at the time that the driver probably thought I was nuts. After talking to lots of tanker drivers since the completion of "Dangerous" I've found it's very common to them. Drivers tell me cars and bikes are always pulling up close to check out their reflections.

The next thought process in "Dangerous" came out of a time crunch. It was now July and at the end of the month I'd be making my annual trek to Sturgis. It's always good to have a painting in progress at a show and this was a big one. It was the 60th anniversary of Sturgis. I wanted to do a painting to commemorate the event but I was involved in this work and don't normally like to work on two paintings at a time. I decided to make "Dangerous" my painting to commemorate the 60th Anniversary of Sturgis. Instead of just doing a 60th Sturgis painting, I'd do one on events that happened at Sturgis and incorporate them into this work. As I set out for Sturgis that year with the truck, trailer, bikes and paintings, I made sure I had a camera full of film. I'd had a plan in mind to have all of my reference materials compiled during the Sturgis road trip. I picked up three significant images on the trip there. In New Mexico I pulled over on an off ramp and photographed a refinery. These reference photos later became the nuclear power plant reflected in the background. In southern Colorado I met a group

At my display during Sturgis you can see the just started "Dangerous" to the left. Carol, one of my spokes-models, is in the white top talking to a customer.

67

of riders heading to Sturgis and asked them to ride along next to me while I shot some photos. These images gave me some shadow reflections off of the bikes and a perspective of bikes in the left lane. Later in Wyoming, and entering the Black Hills, I shot some views of the road and hills and where the vanishing point would appear. I noticed the lack of color in these landscape photos and thought of how I would enhance the colors when I began painting. There are several ways to create the illusion of distance in a flat, two-dimensional painting.

I like to make the items in the foreground more colorful and in focus and the distant background faded and less detailed. All of these elements must be considered before I begin painting.

I arrived at Sturgis late in the afternoon but early in the week because I needed to set up the display. The first night in town you always hook up with old friends and get the feel of the town. Kenny Samson and I went out and he let me crash at his store that evening. Some time later I was awakened to unbelievable weather. Kenny and I ran to the front balcony and a storm like I had never seen whipped through town. Awnings from semis were flying down the road, the hatch on my truck was ripped off, and people were running for cover. Within half an hour the devastation was over and we heard later that it was a tornado. The town of Spearfish got hit pretty badly and the talk all week was about the tornado. Here was another dangerous element (the tornado) to add to the painting that will be remembered by the riders at Sturgis during the 60th. If you look close at the photo of my booth at Sturgis you can see the 'Dangerous' painting in its infancy. Only the trailer is penciled in and I'm starting to paint in some of the basic black areas around the truck. That's

I pulled off I-40 on the way to Sturgis to shoot this refinery which would later become a nuclear power plant reflected in the back of the "Dangerous" semi.

Carol in the halter top, she's one of the spokes-models I use. I also got some photos of the sky the next morning. Clouds are strange moving, visuals. I've found that clouds appear different in various regions of the country. I wanted some funky, threatening, dangerous, Black Hills clouds.

I'm on a roll now and have most of the elements for my painting. I'm still lacking a tractor for the semi though. The tractor photographed in the Beall lot wasn't cool enough for this painting. Once again, things fall in to place. This guy walks in to my booth, says he owns several of my prints and he hauls a chemical tanker. Even better, he has a show-winning semi tractor and it's here at Sturgis. Seems he hooked it up to a trailer and pulled a bunch of his buddy's bikes out from New York. This would never have happened had I not brought along the partially completed painting to

get the crowd's input. Carl and I set up a time before we left Sturgis and he graciously brought his tractor to town so I could photograph it for the painting. He also has a low numbered "Dangerous" print. The tractor was exactly what I needed, a red Peterbuilt. Truckers are a lot like bikers and their equipment is all-important to them. This was an outstanding example of a custom Peterbuilt and I was honored to be able to use it. I photographed the Pete from the angles I needed to draw it into the painting. In all the photographs taken I've always been conscious of the light source. Where is the sun coming from and where will the shadows be cast? While much of the light source can be drawn in later it's always easier to have a good, realistic reference point in your photos.

Man, this painting was just cruising along and

Bikes heading to Sturgis were photographed not just for the view of the motorcycle, but also the shadows they cast upon the highway. All of this time I've been pondering the layout of the painting and how I would position all of the elements within the canvas.

coming together. All of this research, as I like to call it, and so far I've got in less than a week of painting and drawing time. When I get back from Sturgis though, I'm going to have everything I need to wrap up this work. I still needed a bike passing on the left. That shouldn't be hard - I'm at Sturgis. The bike I choose was an awesome chopper built by Rick Fairless in Dallas. Once again, Rick came through and brought the bike by my booth for photography. My friend Scorp posed on the front of the bike and Carol my spokes-model sat on the back. I don't even remember if it was my idea or input from the crowd, but we photographed Carol in a pose as if she was flashing. Notice the guys in the background taking pictures of Carol. When I got back to the studio I placed the bike in a position where it was passing the semi tractor and Carol appears to be flashing the driver. Notice the shadow cast from the bike is at the same perspective of the shadow from the original semi trailer photo.

Time to re-cap, Sturgis is almost over and the photo opportunity is about to end. Got the tractor and trailer, tornado, the makings of a nuclear power plant, passing bike with gal flashing, ominous clouds, Black Hills scenery and vanishing-point perspectives of roads. Good start! Other painting considerations came up along the Sturgis journey but I worked out most of those details in the studio. Items like a South Dakota license plate for the truck and the gals on the mud flaps. Should I have an oncoming vehicle in the passing lane? My sons came up with the plate. I split up the numbering sequence so it wasn't so obvious. C4 4U60 is C4 (the plastic explosive) 4U (for you) 60 is for the 60th anniversary of Sturgis. So these are my ramblings of compiling my reference photos for the painting "Dangerous". Hidden

Long stretches of highway through rolling hills vanishing in the distance. It sounds good on paper, but how do you paint it? You've got to figure that out.

within the painting you'll find these dangerous elements: Tanker hauling dangerous chemicals, me on my Jesse bagger following too close, tornado that hit Sturgis (upper right of tanker) across from a nuclear power plant, (upper left of tanker) trucks throwing rocks, bike passing on a double yellow, (no passing zone) gal on the back of the chopper is flashing the truck driver, the truck is veering in towards the bike to get a better look, road snakes (cracks in the road) and the clouds are getting ominous, (I kind of flamed them). I started the "Dangerous" research in June and it's now September. I'm finally back in the studio with reference materials and it's time to paint. Four months of compiling ideas and photographs from a life on the road. Well worth the time spent on art that will last many lifetimes.

THE PAINTING

It's been a long road and I'm looking forward to the relaxation of painting. As the business of art gets more complex you find you have less time to paint. While the research was fun, I like nothing better than to paint. When at the easel I lose track of time and can paint for eight hours at a stretch. It's like good sex. I begin to pencil in all of my reference material and spend another week working out the details. The perspective of the truck, trailer, and bike were challenging. Both my wife Suzanne, and sons Ian and Dustin have become important critics at this point. Every day they give me their input as the work progresses. Some info I listen to, some I throw out. After the drawing is

complete I will clean it up with a Kneaded eraser and then spray it with a workable fixative.

The production process is similar for most of my paintings. I've found a system that works for me and has given my work a unique style. The dark areas are painted in first, followed by the background colors. The background "effect" was important in this work. The difference between

Carol posing for the photos with the buzzards just waiting for her top to come up. It only came up in the painting.

the clouds in the sky and the clouds reflected in the trailer were important. The same goes for the pavement. The clouds in the sky were not moving as fast as they were in the trailer. I needed to make the vehicles look like they were moving down the road. This was accomplished by elongating the reflections in the trailer. Notice how the clouds curve around the back of the trailer to create some shape. The gravel in the rear of the trailer is in focus at the bottom edge but gets blurred and elongated as it moves toward the top. Follow the double yellow down the side of the trailer and notice how it wraps around the back of the truck. Chrome is the reflection of its surroundings. The horizon line colors are a reflection of the landscape. Notice where the nuclear plant's reflection is, and where it would actually be. Over the viewer's left shoulder. An important but subtle "Dangerous" item was added to the drawing.

Where is the person viewing the painting located? Are you the one on the bike reflected in the truck? The view-point is from the left of the double yellow. The bike reflected in the truck is on your right, slightly ahead of you. You are therefore passing the semi and crowding the tailgating bike. You either have to pass or back off and let the bike over. A subtle but important consideration is where you are placing the person viewing the artwork. In this work it creates some subtle tension and you don't know why.

Not only did I have to deal with surface textures in this work, movement was a concern. A lot of time was spent making the aluminum of the fenders different than the polished stainless of the tank. The same colors were used on both surfaces but painted in a different way. The reflections in the tanker have sharp, hard edges, while the fenders are soft and were painted with a different

Some of the dramatic South Dakota skies photographed for reference. I've been going to Sturgis for fifteen years, and they have some of the wildest storms I've ever seen.

brush. The rims on the truck are polished aluminum. They don't shine as much as the tank, but more than the fenders. On top of that they are moving faster than the rest of the vehicle. You can refer to the reference materials to discover this information, but you have to be able to see it. I guess that's what makes up an artist. If I look at a beautiful sunset, I'm trying to figure out the colors of the sky and how I would paint it. Observation is the key. Every artist has his or her favorite colors to work with, and some they can't stand. I lean towards the turquoise greens and tend to brighten up my colors. I used a lot of blues in the road so the finished painting wasn't 50% grey. Brighter colors are used in the foreground, fading to pastels in the distance. The rocks thrown by the truck have the highest contrast (black & white) with only a small amount of color thrown in. They are the closest item to the viewer. The mountains down the road have the least contrast and eventually fade into white and become the clouds. Notice that the shadows under the trailer and the bike are not black. Dark browns and deep purples were used for the shadows. You can still slightly see the rock texture of the road under the truck. The cracks in the road are large and somewhat detailed in the foreground, but turn in to lines and vanish in the distance.

Wrapping up this work I placed the signature in the foreground, but tried to not make it too dominant. I always know when a painting is finished, and

after six months "Dangerous" was complete. It was shown for the first time, completed, at The Love Ride in Los Angeles. A lot of interest had already been created in this painting just by having it out on the road at several shows. A number of people helped in the creative process and "Dangerous" remains one of my best-known paintings. Prints are still available and the original is in the collection of Samson Exhaust.

The custom Peterbuilt used in the "Dangerous" painting was as trick as any custom bike I've seen. Those individual chromed mud flaps are nostalgia, or now called "old school" look. Very cool.

73

I try not to title my paintings until they're complete, but this one just sings out "High Noon." It's a chopper showdown.

Chapter Eight

High Noon

Cowboy Chopper

For many years now I've created an annual painting for The Laughlin River Run. Laughlin is a gambling town on the Arizona, Nevada, and California border that turns into a motorcycle Mecca each April. I'm familiar with the area and terrain of this high desert landscape as home in Phoenix is only 200 miles away. This year I wanted to portray the small town of Oatman, Arizona. Oatman is a throw back in time and it's a great riding destination while attending Laughlin. Choppers were just starting to come back since the seventies so it was time to do a chopper painting. Master builder Pat Kennedy has been building choppers for as long as I can remember so I thought it only fitting that I paint one of his bikes. Pat and his wife, Brooke, live in Tombstone, Arizona and the western motif of this painting was also fitting. A chopper in Oatman, perfect. A note on Oatman, check out The Oatman Hotel. Clark Gable and Carol Lombard got married there. The roads were dirt at the time, old classic cars, awesome journey. We've posted several dollar bills on the wall of the bar over the years and always find them on our return.

My son Ian and I jumped on the bike and hooked it over to Oatman. It was an overcast day, unusual in the desert, and perfect for taking pictures. Outside of just reference photos, it always helps to experience an area. The sights, smells,

humidity, and aura of an area are reflected better in your work if you experience them first hand. We spent an afternoon in Oatman shooting pho-

Pat Kennedy's chopper was one of the finest examples I have ever seen. Single down tube, no hand controls, mirror molded in to the handlebars, unbelievable.

tos and meeting people. This is time well spent with my boys and I benefit greatly from taking them along. The kids notice things that you overlook. Their minds aren't filled with the clutter that adults have consumed, and they have taught me much. Ian pointed out the rocks and dirt in the road and how it was colored differently than what we were used to. Possibly because it's an old gold mining town. The rock texture in this painting was an important visual effect. I've learned from previous mistakes to not make the background too cluttered. This clutter will detract from the bike. I already had the photos of the chopper I was going to use so I knew what I wanted, I just had to find it. We came across an old building right as you enter town. It was a two

story structure with long vertical lines. I felt like the long lines of the building would enhance the lines of the chopper. The object here was to create some strong visual elements that enhanced the bike and didn't detract from it. A building in the background with horizontal lines would have made the bike look lower and wider. I wanted the Springer front end to look tall and long like it reached the sky. Adding to this illusion of height, I photographed the bike while lying on the ground, shooting up. I also ran the top of the building off the edge of the canvas to create an additional illusion of height.

I sketched in the bike first, adding the building next. Altering the building slightly I made it look like an old saloon with those cool swinging

Oatman reference photos include shots of the rocks, terrain, and burros. You might as well take all you can while you're there. You never know what will end up in the painting.

front doors. The old barn wood had lots of texture and color and was interesting to paint. As in a lot of other materials the wood was built up in layers. There were a surprising amount of blues and grays within the color of the wood. An interesting note here: I sketched out the building and my pencil lines looked good. When I began to paint the building however, something just didn't look correct. It took awhile to figure out what it was. I'm used to painting mechanical objects with exact angles. The building had settled over the years and those uneven angles and lines had created the aged look of the building. My building started out looking like a brand new structure with old barn wood. I had to make a conscious effort to create crooked lines and non symmetrical shapes. The faded word 'Saloon' was dry brushed in using a muted red like it had faded in years of sunlight. The background was difficult for me in several ways. The angles didn't sit right in my mind and I usually don't work in browns. They're not my favorite color. I wanted to force myself to work with these colors so my body of work had some variety. Even though you may paint different angles of bikes and different models, you will naturally be attracted to the bikes and colors you like. Years ago I had a customer point out the fact that all my paintings had drag bars. He was right. I'm a drag bar guy and usually run them on my bikes. Likewise, I've since made a conscious effort to mix up the selection of handlebars and bike styles within my paintings. The

Photos taken of the old building in "High Noon" show how out of square all the woodwork is and how the building has settled over the years.

sky was a washed out pastel blue as will happen in bright sunlight. If I had dropped in a bright blue it would have pulled your attention to the sky, which is not where I wanted it. Once again, composition and eye movement are crucial to a good piece of art. The person viewing the art may not understand this, they'll just enjoy the work. I see more capable motorcycle artists that can render the subject effectively but they don't have a clue about composition, color, and eye movement. These are some of the tools that a college education offers an artist. Invaluable.

Moving from the building to the ground I analyzed the photos of the rocks my son had pointed out. I built the ground up in layers, first laying down a large area of blue/grey and then added the rocks on top. The blue/grey mix was brushed on horizontally and some brown was added in the distance as it nears the building. While the basis of the ground was grey, the rocks on top were brown. As your eye views the terrain on the ground these two colors will blend in the distance. The rocks are more detailed, colorful, and have more contrast in the foreground than they do in the background. The shadow under the bike is a mix of the same color used in the brown of the rocks. Added to this I threw in some pebbles stuck in the tires. Living in Arizona I've noticed how when it's hot and tires get soft they tend to pick up more rocks. It's a nice little touch, adds some detail, and brings your attention to the tire which is in the foreground. The

If you have ever been to Oatman this building is instantly recognizable at it's the largest building as you enter town. It's a work of art in its own right.

grays and browns of the ground were important in this work, as those would be the colors reflected in the bike. There wasn't much blue in the sky to use on the metallic surfaces of the bike. Pat Kennedy doesn't use a lot of chrome in his bikes and prefers to use polished aluminum and stainless steel where possible. I kept these considerations in mind when selecting my background colors.

Working on the bike I moved to the sheet metal first. I altered the colors of the bike as I felt the red/violet suited the painting better than the original orange color. I don't remember when the title developed, but being "High Noon" meant I had to put the light source over head. The high-

lights on the tank and the shadow underneath the bike reflect the angle of the sun. The painting of the bike was straightforward and I followed the sequence that works for me moving from darks to lights. Care was taken to differentiate surfaces like the polished aluminum versus the chrome. Areas like the magneto and front brake rotor were painted the blue/gray of the ground, and a dry brush technique of browns was added to the top. This effect added to the overall color and reflected the colors from the rocks below. The front wheel was a bitch. Between the spokes and dual disc brakes, I thought I was never going to finish. Added to that I had a deadline because the Laughlin folks were using this piece for the cover of their catalog.

What a cool creative place. Old mining machinery, tractors, old buildings, guy stuff.

I finished the painting on time, the Laughlin folks were happy, the original sold for big bucks, and the prints are consistent sellers. What is not apparent is all the knowledge, effort, and research this or any other painting takes. While I love my job and find it enjoyable to paint, many projects are completed in long sleepless nights or waking at 3:00 AM to begin painting. Try holding a palette in front of you, or your brush hand extended and clenched for twelve-hour days. Cramped muscles, sleepless nights, packing and loading paintings and bikes, and then driving 30 hours to the next bike event. Not how I envisioned my artistic career before I started it. There have been a lot of miles put on over the years to create and get my artwork out to the public.

That's all part of the gig. One day you're in a corporate jet and comped suites at the Hilton, the next you're sleeping in your truck on the road to Daytona for Bike Week. The whole experience will add depth to my artwork as it evolves over the years. One of the most frequently asked questions is, "how long did this painting take you?" The answer: my whole life. The painting process is only part of the whole picture. On one painting, and I don't recall if it was this one, I decided to keep track of the hours in the painting process. Every day as I painted, I logged the hours on a note pad. After two or three days I noticed I would paint six to ten hours a day, and then sit back and look at the work, sometimes two or three hours a day. You need this time to analyze

A must stop is the bar at the Oatman Hotel. Tell them the bike artist and Ms. Budweiser sent you.

the project and see where you are going to take it. Should I log these hours spent looking and not painting? I was just sitting there drinking beer looking at my art, but it's not like I was out riding. The painting needed this time to develop. The whole log-book of hours got more frustrating, and seemed like stupid paperwork, so I dropped it. I now look at year's end and see how many paintings I've completed. Some years up to five, some only two. When I get down to two a year, even if they're grand and require a lot of research, I make an effort to spend more time painting. Some artists are required, usually by their publishers, to crank out lots of paintings. I've known artists who were required to knock out up to six works a month. There's a point where the art will suffer greatly from this desire for greed. Good art takes time and cannot be dictated by anyone but the artist. This is one of the reasons I've decided over the years to do my own thing and not be encumbered by agents or art publishing companies. You may make more money at first, but I feel your career may be short lived as your art deteriorates because someone is now telling you how many and in what colors.

As soon as the sales of your art slow many publishers will drop you like a hot potato and grab the next new talent or trend. Beware. It's all about the Art. No matter how long it takes.

The original painting is in the collection of Tim Voltz.

A view looking through town with the mountains going up in to the clouds. We take for granted things like buried utility lines when they used to clutter up the scenery.

Chapter Nine

The Afterburn

Jet Powered Harleys

I guess I kind of see my job as not only a motorcycle artist but as an historian of sorts. When the tragedy of 911 struck us I felt compelled to do a painting. I didn't want to bring up the tragedy or look like I was capitalizing on this horrible event so I thought about our armed forces and the motorcycle community. A lot of bikers I know and ride with are Vietnam and Desert Storm veterans. You'll find bikers are the first ones to step up in time of need. I wanted to create an image of the motorcyclist and service man going to kick some ass.

"The Afterburn" a pilots' view from an F-16. A scene only a select few will ever see but we would all like to experience. The awesome power behind the U.S. Military Forces.

Pondering this latest painting challenge I recalled several incidents that have happened to me. Twice in my lifetime I've been riding along and out of nowhere a fighter jet sneaks up behind and strafes me. Talk about power and scaring the daylights out of you. I'm sure the pilots did it on purpose and it certainly was effective. I also live in Phoenix where the largest F-16 training base in the world is located. Compiling all this visual information I wondered what the pilots view from above, looking down on the bikes, would look like? That was it - an F-16 fighter jet, from above, with a pack of bikers going to kick some ass. This was going to be interesting. I know very little about planes and don't really like to fly. As usual I set out to compile my reference photos beginning with something I know, bikes.

The reference photos taken of the bikes were more to establish some angles. The bikes would be at a distance and painting the details would not be as crucial as in most of my paintings. The angles were going to be different because you are not normally looking down on a motorcycle from 500 feet above. I found an area at a local bike shop where I could get to the three-story roof next door. Lining up six of the mechanics from the shop in club formation (side by side) I walked along the roof and took photos looking down as if I were in a plane. It was kind of interesting to walk past the stationary bikes and see how the perspective changed. Normally the bikes would be passing you, the stationary object. In a small way I started to visualize what a pilot would see. Turning my head sideways when

Bikes lined up in club formation and photographed from the roof of a building for the "Afterburn". The bagger in the second row was manned by Brownie, a decorated Vietnam vet and friend who we lost recently. Missed, but not forgotten.

shooting the photos also threw the horizon at an angle. It was like when you're taking a fast turn on a bike the horizon line will go to a 45-degree angle.

Back in the studio I started to pencil in my imaginary road and the scene from above. This was a weird angle to work from. I decided to turn the rectangular canvas on a 45-degree angle and see if that worked. Putting the lower right corner of the canvas at the bottom of my easel I secured it with C-Clamps on a 45. The horizon line was now level and I could pencil in the formation of bikes. I turned the canvas back and forth to normal several times and this was starting to work. A little aside: A trick I learned in art school to check proportions and perspective helped me out here. If you have a large mirror,

look at your artwork in the mirrored image. I don't know why, it's not just the amplified distance created by the mirror, but it's much easier to note any proportion or perspective adjustments. This mirror trick works and I use it frequently.

I've got the bikes going down the road, the horizon is at a 45, and a new thought struck me. How about incorporating an American flag into the background. Since this painting is about American fighting men, I need a flag. Painting in some sand dunes on the right side of the road gave an illusion of stripes. On the left I'd paint an orchard of trees and make them kind of star shaped. This took some refinement later but the end result is a subtle American flag created in the background of the landscape. Some of the stuff I

Lt. Col. Moondawgie checking out the specifics at my studio. I like the ink Moon, is that Air Force issue?

hide in my artwork I don't know if anyone will notice. I've come to the realization that it doesn't matter. I think it's kind of cool and enjoyed the challenge of trying to pull it off. I continued to first paint in the background and sky to establish my colors. If you observe a sky from top to bottom, and analyze the colors, you'll notice there's purple at the top of the frame, fading down through blue-green, to almost white at the horizon line. Sometimes this change of colors is more dramatic than others, but it always exists. The rate of change in colors of the sky is important in creating the desired amount of distance you will be establishing in your painting.

At this point I needed to get some reference photos of an F-16 fighter jet. If I would have known how tough this was going to be I may not have started this painting. Added to this challenge "The Afterburn" was started only three weeks after 911 and the country was on edge. We tried the internet and didn't get too far. There were lots of sites but cockpits were blacked out and there was not enough detail for what I needed. My marketing assistant, Jenny, contacted the Public Relations Department at Luke Air Force Base and while they were cordial, they couldn't be bothered at this point in time. This was totally understandable. The painting gets put on hold and I start to put out feelers to everyone I know that I need some F-16 reference material. The motorcycle show season was to begin soon, starting with Bike Week in Daytona. I'd take the partially completed painting along and see who I'd meet and what developed. There was a lot of interest generated

Cockpit reference photos taken in Tucson. The stick with all the weapons is on the right, ejection handle sits between your legs, appropriate.

in this work and I even had several offers to purchase the painting before it was finished, but it took several shows before I met 'Moondawgie.'

Hanging out in my booth at Arizona Bike Week this dude walks up and says, "what have you got going on here?" I explain what I'm trying to do while he cocks his head and just stares at the partially finished canvas. He pulls out a business card, hands it to me, and introduces himself as 'Moondawgie' an F-16 pilot. My new best friend. Moon is based out of Tucson, only an hour away and invites me to the base to get the reference pictures I need. Even better, he asks if I want to go up for a flight, or in the simulator? Hell yes. We exchange numbers, and he schedules a time. Then my ten-year old son Dustin and I pack up the camera, the painting, and head to Tucson. Greeted at the gate of The Air National Guard complex in Tucson by a gentleman with an automatic

Pilot's view from inside an F-16. An incredibly tight fit. You are also reclined at a 45 degree angle which would seem uncomfortable for long periods. I asked "Moon" what was the longest he has been in the cockpit for a stretch, and he answered "twelve hours."

weapon, we were waved on through. This 'Moondawgie' dude must be for real cause we didn't even stop. Either that or I was mudchecked before I got there and didn't know it. Dustin and I follow an escort to an area where we were asked to load in to a S.W.A.T. type vehicle and 'Moon' would meet us out on the flight line. Unbelievable. After all this time my son and I are standing on the flight line with 75 F-16s. 'Moondawgie' allowed us to climb into an F-16, take our reference photos, and explained the tools of his trade. Bonus points - the public relations people of the Guard unit show up and photograph Dustin and I for an article they want to do. We spend an hour with 'Moon', get an education and then it's time for the simulator. We rumble off to another building in the

SW.A.T. van and we enter a room with main frame computers that look like something out of NASA. There are two F-16 cockpits, like sections of a plane, sitting in the middle of all this computer hardware. Very Cool! 'Moon' climbs in, shows us how to work the basic controls, and then brings the simulator to the exact height and bank angle as my roughed in painting. He asks the computer operator to freeze the image and then says, "climb in Eric." I got to see the exact angle from the correct bank and altitude for the painting. I was pretty close in my original drawing but what I noticed was how flat the trees and verticals in the terrain appeared. I would have to alter the bikes slightly and make them larger than they would actually appear from 500 feet.

After that I was allowed to fly in the simula-

Lt. Col. Moondawgie, Eric Herrmann and the painting in it's infancy - with seventy five F-16s.

tor for 45 minutes. Rolls, banks, crashes, I got to experience it all. No photographs were allowed at this time. It was information overload. I know the controls and gauges on a bike, but not being a pilot, I didn't have a clue. I found myself paying too much attention to the gauges and where they would be set when I should have been flying. An awesome experience, and Dustin at ten years old was also allowed to fly. "Moon" let him shoot the guns (I wasn't allowed) and he stuck the landing when I crashed several times. It was a great experience for a little man. I was more concerned with the visuals of the cockpit. How the gauges would be set and the lighting on the instruments. One thing that stuck in my mind as I climbed out wobbly-legged is how your senses can be altered by your sight. The cockpit wasn't on hydraulics and never moved. Only the scenery on the plasma screens around you moved. I would have bet money I was moving at least a little. Dustin and I took 'Moon' to Hooters for dinner, thanked him, and headed to Phoenix with an "I'll be in touch with more questions" good-bye.

The photos turned out great and I was able to pencil in the cockpit with a confident degree of accuracy. Outside of the photos my visual knowledge had greatly expanded, experiencing imagery at 600 knots. I started to paint in the details of the cockpit leaving most of the gauges blank. Over the next few months I had a lot of questions for "Moon" on where specific gauges should be set and how to place the markings on the HUD (Heads up Display). "Moon" went out of his way and worked with me e-mailing specifics and stopping by every few weeks to make sure it was technically accurate. I got quite

> **Rolls, banks, crashes, I got to experience it all...it was information overload.**

an education and we added specifics that only fighter pilots may understand. The pilots left hand is on the throttle and jamming it into the after-burn position. When an F-16 hits the after-burner the exhaust is emitted in a ring formation as noticed by the shadow cast on the ground. All of the gauges were correctly positioned and the Guard people told me it was the most accurate rendition of a cockpit they had ever seen. Certain artistic liberties were taken like the motorcycle gloves worn by the pilot. The canopy that covers the cockpit is a specialized UV glass and when in the plane you don't even see glass. No reflections, nothing. I gave an indication of the canopy by altering the texture of the clouds.

The cockpit took a lot of time. It wasn't difficult to paint, mostly grey and slight amounts of color, but the accuracy with which it had to be drawn was comparable to drawing a motorcycle engine. Notice the flight suit has some golds in the grey to differentiate it from the metallic surroundings. I also used some night-time photos of the cockpit with the gauges glowing so I could dub in some color. There are very subtle changes in the grays of the cockpit. Some blue grays, some dark grays, to create some depth and texture. When I first started roughing in the grays I started with a shade in the middle, a 50% if you will. This way I could move toward light or dark grey always referring back to the middle gray. When rendering an item like this cockpit, establish in your mind the lightest, darkest, and middle tones of the entire area. Move laterally as you paint, always referring back to your baseline.

With the cockpit 90% complete I began moving around the painting. Starting to tighten up the bikes, I decided to incorporate various important insignias on the back of the bikers. They include: the American Flag (out front), the 195th fighter squadron, the Chicago Flag, the Arizona Flag with ANG (Air National Guard), a POW-MIA shirt so we never forget - and an American Flag bringing up the rear. You'll also find the bikers packing sawed off shotguns and 12-inch-barrel 357s. I threw in an assortment of bike models including: a bagger, a custom, a Road King, a Dyna, and an FXR. Rounding out the painting I decided to put more stars and stripes hidden in the clouds, and also put Moon's name in there for all his help. The last thing I needed to do was to create some movement. I thought I'd blur out some of the scenery so it would look like a pilot's view. This proved a little more challenging than originally expected. If I blurred the background from a point at the nose of the jet, then the F-16 would be going straight ahead. The way the painting is viewed, the F-16 is banking to the right. I selected a point on the horizon line where the plane was headed and blurred items in the foreground off of that point. Items in the foreground are blurred more than subjects in the distance.

While they weren't the last items to be painted in they deserve some attention. During my F-16 education I learned that the pilots could only see the ground if they were on a 45 degree bank. I wanted to cast some shadows of the F-16's to confirm what type of cockpit this was in front of you. To get the shadows correct we went to the store and purchased

a model of an F-16. My son Ian assembled it and we hung it from a ladder with a light source above (the light source in this painting is over the pilot's left shoulder). With the model plane angled on a 45 it cast a shadow, a shadow that became part of my painting. "Moondawgie" even figured out which direction the plane was flying to match the shadows and incorporated that into the compass in the cockpit. Thanks to everyone who helped out on this work. There were a lot of people and hours involved but the end result was worth the effort. I have a whole different appreciation for the military and I'm honored that "The Afterburn" prints hang in military bases all over the world. The original painting is in the collection of Dave Huntzinger, a world-renowned aviation safety expert.

Moondawgie and my son Dustin hanging out with 75 F-16's. What an awesome experience for an eleven year old.

Chapter Ten

Crank'n

High Speed Canvas

"Crank'n" was my first painting of this nature, a rider's perspective, a view over the handlebars if you will. I wanted to get the feeling of riding a motorcycle across to the person viewing the artwork. It's a challenging perspective, but bikers understand it instantly. It took some work but "Crank'n" has remained one of my best selling prints and the entire print edition is close to being sold out.

My original concept was not just to create a rider's perspective, but to incorporate one of those unique instances that happen when you're riding - at least if you ride the way my friends and I do. If you'll notice in the mirror there is a

I almost titled "Crank'n" Oh-Shit. Why is it whenever you get on the throttle, a cop pops up in your mirror?

police car. It is also a flat stretch of road with no side roads. How come whenever you think you can get on it, a cop pops up out of nowhere? So I had my job cut out for me.

I started with finding the correct bike. I wanted a monster - a fire breathing hot rod. I located a proto-type built by Pure Steel that had something like 180 Horsepower with Nitrous Oxide boost and the whole nine yards. The bike itself was too busy of a subject to paint but the handlebar setup was perfect for what I was after. The monster tach from Auto Meter was new to the market and this was the first bike I had seen it used on. I began this painting with only the photos of the bike. Photographing the handlebar set-up I intentionally cocked them slightly. If you notice when you're riding, especially at speed, you are constantly adjusting and rarely

are your bars in a straight line, especially if you're banging a gear or two. All of the details like the squad car, background, and arms came later. With only the bike penciled in I headed for Sturgis. You can see by the photos in my booth, I painted in the black and was just starting to add in the color on the tach. Notice how I pegged it at 7000 RPM. The little red light is a shift light that lights up and tells you when to shift when you're racing. The little chip on the light can be changed for different RPMs, with this one set at 6800.

Working on the bars first I brightened up the colors. The photographs were shot indoors and there was no reflected color from the sky or the surroundings. I knew when I completed this piece it would be "Crank'n" down a highway somewhere under a bright blue sky. The bars

"Crank'n" reference photo showing the Monster Auto Meter Tach which I took some artistic liberties with and pegged at seven grand. Some of the design elements of the bike are old news now but were cutting edge at the time. The tach, flush mounted gas cap, levers, lines running through the triple trees...Builders, designers, and artists keep pushing the envelope to create new and better products for the consumer.

and tach took some serious time to paint. Everything in the foreground of a painting is clearer, more detailed and in focus. I wanted to do that beautiful Auto Meter tach some justice. The cover was on the shift light when photographed so that was added in using bright red to appear like it was lit up. Notice what I call speed marks or wisps of white coming from the bar ends, mirror, and master cylinder covers. While you never see these except if you're in a jet, they add to the illusion of speed. I've been painting bikes for quite some time now and know most of the manufacturers of parts and accessories. The master cylinders are Jay Brakes, made by my friend and wild man, Jay. Whenever I'm reproducing someone's parts and logos in my paintings I try to do them justice and take the same care they have taken in designing and producing the parts. In certain industries it may be frowned upon to reproduce someone's logo. I've found the motorcycle industry to be extremely accommodating, and often going out of their way to help me. I completed the bars before moving on to the rest of the background. The knurled handgrips were rendered in completely, even though I knew most of them would be covered up with the rider's hands. By doing this, the knurling on both sides of each hand matches up and doesn't look like it was dubbed in later. Sometimes it's best to think in layers even though parts will get covered up later. This was the case

Arms on the bars, a view we see daily as riders, but without a visual reference becomes difficult if not impossible to paint accurately.

with the hand grips. While this bike had Nitrous it never occurred to me to put the riders thumb on the Nitrous button. While I was at Sturgis someone said, "Hey, you ought to put his thumb on the juice button." I don't even remember who threw that out there, but thanks. It's a nice touch. It's one more example of the good things that happen when you're painting out in public. You can get ideas from other people and take credit for them.

I had photographs of the builder's arms, Phil, but I didn't have a good shot of a hand with the thumb extended out. Jumping on the bike I rode to a local dealership and shot Bill's thumb extended to the nitrous button, wearing a set of my riding gloves. I faded the arms in to

a black t-shirt that was just slightly darker than the black of the pavement. Once again, on the white stripes of the road I added my speed lines to create movement. I now had the arms, hands, road, and the whole portion of the bike painted. I needed a squad car for the mirror and a background.

Once again, it just blows me away how things work out. I grabbed my camera and headed over to the local Phoenix Police station several miles from my home. I explained who I was through the bullet-proof glass window and how I needed a reference photo of a cop car. I was introduced to Detective Larry Santa Cruz who asked me what kind of car I needed. A cop car is a cop car. They're all the same and have

I positioned my vehicle to get that scary sight in the left side mirror. Only this one's more terrifying, a pro-street hood scoop.

flashing lights on the top. Well, Larry took me to the motor pool area and proceeded to pull out a pro street squad from a three axle Featherlight trailer. As it turns out, there's a whole series of Drag Racing Police cars and this is one of the first. I have an 800 horsepower squad in my rear view mirror. Perfect! They lined up the car, named Blue By You, turned on the lights, and I photographed it in the rear view mirror of my truck. I promised them several low number prints upon completion of the painting and they flipped my five-year old son a cool t-shirt. Nice guys. I also got to add a nice police touch that, I would have never known, but is often picked up by law enforcement bikers at the events. The 510 on the front plate of the squad car is a Phoenix Police code for a speeding vehicle. They have several low number prints and I'm told one is hanging in the police chief's office. When the car went to the nationals they came by for "Crank'n" t-shirts for the pit crew. Eric got a "get out of jail" pass as they know my bikes and I've never been pulled over since. I love the perks of this job.

The last detail of this painting was the background. I needed somewhere out in the open. No side roads, no distractions. It was now the end of August and I was headed to the Four Corners Rally in southern Colorado. It's an eight-hour ride from Phoenix across four corners and some barren Indian Reservation land. A wide-open ride where you can really get on it

"Crank'n" in my booth at Sturgis when I was just beginning to get some paint laid down. Ron Simms loaned me one of his latest creations to help class the place up. I always wanted to paint that bike, in a setting, perhaps a southern mansion, behind a large ornamental iron gate. Last I saw of that bike it was red and looked completely different. Nice bike.

and clear your head out. I didn't plan on it, once again it just happened, and I came upon the perfect background to complete "Crank'n." I found blue skies, nice golden browns of the high desert, and the colors worked well with the painting. I noticed how the clouds out in the wide-open spaces fade away and become indistinguishable from the mountains in the distance. The colors of the desert also changed as they moved away from the rider. While you can see some green in the bushes close to the rider these colors fade and lose their color in the distance. I added in the barbed wire fence to create the illusion of no side roads and no places for the squad to hide. I originally had the thought of putting a hot gal on the right side of the road hitchhiking. Kind of like the biker had to make a decision like, "should I stay or should I go?" I nixed that idea because she would have been small and blurry if she was in the foreground.

The original "Crank'n" painting has been sold several times and is currently in the collection of Samson Exhaust. The original canvas is available for $48,000.00. One of the most unique compliments I get on my artwork is when a biker comes up to me at a show and says, "I've had your painting tattooed on my back." This has happened several times with different works of art, "Crank'n" is one of them.

During Bike Week I met this dude with "Crank'n" inked on his back. I don't have any tattoos, but one year a guy up in Laconia gave me a quickie how-to lesson. It's a much more difficult art form than it appears and I think I'll stick with my brushes and stationary canvas. Lots of respect.

It's all about the details. That's what makes "Shovelheat" a success. The details of the bike, the fireworks, the rocks. It's the details, man.

Chapter Eleven

Shovel Heat

Classy Classic

"Shovelheat" didn't start out as the desire to paint a Shovelhead motor, but with the intention of an event painting. I'd been attending the Laconia Rally and Races in New Hampshire for several years and Laconia was getting ready to celebrate its 75th Anniversary. A lot of people don't realize this, but the Laconia event has been around longer than the Sturgis Black Hills Rally and Daytona's Bike Week. I'd met the event organizers and threw out the idea of an official painting to help celebrate their 75th and they loved it. This event is different from the other bike runs and hasn't gotten as commercialized. There are a lot of hard-core riders on the east coast and it shows at Laconia. These are the riders that don't care about the rain or even the snow. Cool. So after going to Laconia for several years and checking out the bikes I noticed there was a difference in the bikes as well as the people. Never had I seen so many Shovelheads and Sportsters. Talking with an old friend, Scott, from New York, I decide to paint a Shovelhead. Now I don't take the decision to paint a particular bike lightly. My paintings

take a long time and I will only be able to paint a select few in my lifetime. So Shovelhead it was, and it also turned out to be the right decision. While everyone at the time was riding Evolution

The original flame color on this Shovelhead sure looked good against the Arizona desert, but the correct color change was made to match the background of the painting.

motors, when I began riding it was Shovelheads. Most of the riders in my age bracket began on Shovelheads or Panheads. This painting had to have a harder edge to reflect the Laconia event and the New England riders.

I got on the phone back in Phoenix and called all the local shops to see what kind of Shovelheads they had around. Paul Yaffe, an exceptional builder, had a '75 Shovelhead in a rigid frame he had just re-done for a customer. I jumped on the scooter and rode down to Paul's place to check it out. I've seen a lot of Paul's work and he has a good design sense for what a particular bike should be. This was the perfect version of a Shovelhead for my Laconia painting. Drag bars and pipes, short bobbed fender, flames - a rowdy

little Shovelhead. I shot some photos of the bike and found out later that a professional photographer friend, Butch, had also shot the bike for one of the bike magazines. Butch allowed me to use several of his photos and the clarity of the photographs definitely helped the painting. I decided on a 3/4 rear view to show off the rear tire and pipe side of the bike. This tends to be one of my favorite angles for viewing a bike, and I have to be careful not to use it too often.

I started laying out this work as I usually do, penciling in the bike and painting the black first. Black bikes are difficult to paint as it is harder to see the shapes and reflections on a black painted surface than it is on lighter colors. Here's where the clarity of the photographs helped immensely.

The famous Weirs Beach sign and the annual motorcycle madness. Laconia, it's different from the rest, if it's not raining.

This painting was one of my larger ones with an overall canvas size of 52 x 60 inches. The painting was just beginning, and I was headed for Laconia so I took it with and worked on it while at the show. This gave me important feedback and also allowed me to get the other necessary elements that I needed to make it the official painting. The Weirs Beach sign is probably the most recognizable element from the Laconia event, and the fireworks display that highlights the rally is always a crowd favorite. I decided to incorporate them into the painting. One of the stipulations the event promoters had was that I use the official logo somewhere in the painting. I came up with the idea of putting it on a patch on a leather jacket lying on the ground. I wanted to make this work appear as if you got off the bike, threw your jacket on the ground, pulled off your goggles, and sat back to watch the fireworks and check out your scooter. The official logo is on the jacket as well as the NASWA resort logo, which is a landmark in the area. Check out the NASWA if you're in the Weirs Beach area. The Makris family is very hospitable and the homemade desserts are unbelievable. These slight little elements like the Laconia patch and the Naswa resort logo, lend credibility to your work as riders know you've been there and are not just faking the con-

cepts. Put the extra effort in to your work, do the research, make it real, and the benefits will come. I have two different groups of customers that now buy this print. One bunch buys it because it's a Shovelhead, the other purchases it because it represents the Laconia rally.

As the painting progressed elements changed

One of my old worn out leathers from the seventies used as a prop. It's not like you can fit into them anymore, but you can't throw them away either.

as usual. I decided to change the flame colors on the original bike from a yellow to a magenta color. This color would be easier to tie in to the fireworks colors I had envisioned. Care had to be taken to not make the flames pink. I had to pull off this rowdy Shovelhead painting without making it too feminine. Part of how that was accomplished was by pinstriping the flames in a contrasting blue. When opposite colors on the color wheel of the same intensity are used they appear to vibrate. This vibration of colors is generally not a good visual effect but it can be carefully manipulated to achieve certain results. It can work well on flames as it leaves the tips looking hot. The blue border of pinstriping against the magenta (dark pink) makes your eye see the edge of the flames as

a purple. I know I did my job because over the years I've had a number of bikers tell me they painted their bikes to match my "Shovelheat" painting. Another item added was the leaves lying on the ground. The brown of the leaves contrasted well with the blue of the rocks. When I decided to add the leaves I looked around and all I had available were the wimpy tree leaves we have in the Phoenix desert. I called my brother Carl, who lives in the New England area, and asked him to go out in the back yard and grab some old fallen leaves and send me a bunch. It's interesting how a model, or prop, like these leaves can help with a painting. Holding the actual leaf in your hand, and being able to turn it and see the veins running through it is so much more valuable than a photo-

Fireworks over the lake as viewed from the NASWA resort during the Laconia Motorcycle Rally and Races.

graph. The leaves were painted in, the jacket with the patches was on the ground, but I needed a little more. I decided to work up the rocks around the bike. I left indentations like the ground was soft as the bike rolled through them. Care was taken to figure out the light and shadows cast by the fireworks upon the rocks. Notice how there is a little more light shining around the front tire than hidden behind it.

Painting the fireworks was a bitch. I had some photographs of fireworks, but being an amateur photographer at best, didn't leave me with quality reference material. As the fireworks display began I sat on the pier at the NASWA overlooking the lake. The one part I was lacking were the smoke trails from where the fireworks were launched. I added those in to the painting and it helped. I want to try and paint more fireworks as it turned out to be much more difficult than I had imagined. I guess it's like painting fire, the motion is hard to capture in a static piece of artwork.

"Shovelheat" took me longer to complete than any previous painting. While I normally work on only one painting at a time, I had several other projects going on while I was completing this work. There became

some obvious pros and cons to working on more than one piece at a time. I also had a year to finish this painting as it didn't need to be done till the 75th. You know how that goes. It didn't get completed until just in time. The advantage of taking so long to complete this work was that it sat at

Aviator goggles strapped to the bars of my custom bike "Suds". Note how they are on the right side of the bars. If placed on the left they would slide off, and a biker would know this and never put his goggles on the low side. A small item like this could blow the entire credibility of a motorcycle work of art.

different stages of completion in my studio. I was able to analyze it, work out details in color and composition, and in general it became a better painting because of the time spent looking at it. The downside was I would not have the time to paint on it for several week stretches. When I would go back to painting I'd have to get in the groove. I'd forgotten what colors I'd mixed to get certain details. It became even more time consuming than it should have been. The correct balance of painting time and analysis time has to be struck to create a great painting. You can't just knock them out. You have to spend time looking at your work. Figure out what needs to be added, fixed, or altered. You also need to keep the project moving forward without too much down time. You'll get stagnant and lose interest unless you see the progress. Kind of like writing this book.

"Shovelheat" was completed shortly before the 75th Anniversary of Laconia, and was shown for the first time at Harley-Davidson's 95th Anniversary celebration. It was sold immediately to a favorite collector, Dan Bishop. I should probably add some information about the value of collectors to an artist. When I started painting I never thought about collectors or who was going to buy my artwork. I was just going to paint and see what happened. I've also never had a problem with letting a piece go or selling it. I just move on to the next project. A couple of years into my art career I started to get some notoriety and my work started showing up more frequently in magazines.

One of my Laconia friends hanging out with the just started "Shovelheat". I was given one of the famous HOG Farm shirts and wore it proudly until it wore out.

Dan is an avid art collector and truly enjoys art. He's also ridden for over 30 years. We crossed paths at Daytona many years ago and he purchased a painting from me. Over the years he has purchased a number of original paintings. He has sold some, made some money, and introduced me to a number of new clients. Over the years we have become good friends. Collectors, patrons of the arts, friends, whatever you want to call them are invaluable to an artist's career. I didn't know when Dan bought that first painting from me just how much he helped me to further my art career. When I am sold out of paintings, and have a show, he is always there to loan me an original to display. I value his input and appreciate what collectors like Dan and Kenny Samson have done for me and my artwork. They are not just rich guys who have the money to buy art, but truly appreciate the artwork. They have helped my career in so many ways I can't count. As an artist, I hope you run across people of this caliber during your career. My life and art are better because of them. Thank You.

"Shovelheat" gets some road time, in and travels from New Hampshire to Los Angeles for the grand opening of a new store. While painting on location at Pujol, I noticed a ten year old girl watching me intently. I asked her if she wanted to paint. For a good hour she painted under my direction and did an outstanding job. A week later I received a thank you letter from the girl and her dad. I packed up a bunch of old brushes, and unused paint and shipped them to her. It sure made me feel good and I hope she's still painting.

Chapter Twelve

Gettin' Lucky

Hookin' it out of Town

"Gettin' Lucky" was one of my annual paintings for the Laughlin River Run event. As the official artist I create a painting each year to document or show my version of what Laughlin has to offer the biker. Like most bikers, I have a problem with authority or people telling me what to do. The folks that put on the Laughlin event pretty much give me free rein, so I enjoy

I just love that shit-eatin' grin on John's face and Jeannie's flamed hair.

doing these annual paintings. When I started painting full time I made the conscious decision to paint what I wanted. If you like it fine. If you don't, I don't really care. Up to this point in time I'd been involved in the commercial end of the art business. Working with corporations, board decisions, etc. There is nothing more frustrating to an artist than to have some corporate geek change or alter your artwork when you know the best solution to the project. So I have some general guidelines, but it's not like the promoters tell me what to do.

A number of photos were taken of my models and combined to get the feeling I was after...

...I like to use friends and real bikers in my paintings - after all, why use strangers when you've got the real thing?

Laughlin is a gambling town and I needed to get that across in this painting. It's also on the Arizona, Nevada, border and has a Western, or cowboy, flair to it. People often bring up the fact that the biker is a modern day cowboy. Well I don't know about that, but I guess there are some similarities. I thought I'd try to get that point across, a modern day biker, against an old western setting. I also had to capture the gambling flavor of Laughlin. So I was setting myself up for a fantasy piece. I decided to go all the way and have a biker that wins it all. Wins all the money, gets the hot chick, and hooks it out of town evading all the bad guys. Kind of like an old Western movie.

I started by rounding up two biker friends John and Jeannie to use for models. I had already ridden over to Laughlin and photographed some of the casinos for the backdrop. The Pioneer Casino worked well as it was made up to look like an old western town. So at this point in time I already had a vision in my head of what I wanted the painting to look like. I envisioned a Western town in the background - and the biker getting out of Dodge with the chick and all the loot. I started to round up my photographs and put the pieces of the puzzle together. I took a number of photos of John and Jeannie on a chopper, and at some point in time asked John to put his shades down on his nose and give me a shit eatin' grin. I also wanted that big hair thing and they both had it

An excuse to jump on the bike and ride over to Laughlin. Hey Suzanne, I'll be gone for a few days - working on a painting. What a gal!

106

going on. It's important to know at this point I was planning ahead, and had brought some props to the photo shoot to make my painting job easier. I specifically found a chopper with a sissy bar so I could put a bedroll on the back. Nevada is a helmet state but I wanted the helmet on the back. There are also these huge Margarita glasses at Laughlin, and you can walk around with your mega cocktail and maybe make it home with one of the glasses. I rounded up one to strap on the sissy bar as well. By this point I had the basics to begin

I never knew they used Clydesdales to pull wagons and stagecoaches. I'll have to watch some old westerns and check it out.

The stagecoach was a trip. Different size wheels and suspension that consisted of leather straps that worked wet or dry.

the background photos of the Laughlin casinos and the bikers in the foreground headed for Arizona.

I began painting by establishing my background colors and painting in the sky and mountains. From there I moved to the casino buildings. As I painted the buildings, I intentionally tried to age them to make them look a little more like an old western town. I roughed up the stucco on the front of the Pioneer and toned down the colors a bit. Knowing I would go back to the buildings to add people and horses later, I only worked up this area to 80% completion. From there I moved to the bikers in the foreground. The faces and hair came along and there wasn't a whole lot of bike to paint, but certain areas took some time. I wanted the leathers to look old and dusty, and the

jeans to be worn and faded. The gold tones of the sand in the background were worked into the leathers to create the worn look. Care was taken to give Jeannie the perfect breasts with just the nipples touching John's back. I love this job. While I photo-graphed the bikers standing still, I had to create some movement and get Jeannie's hair flowing. As it extended out I decided to flame it and created a flame pattern with her hair. After all, this was a fantasy piece. I could do whatever I wanted. Working up the bike and figures I began adding the gambling influences. In John's left glove you'll notice several $100 bills. Stuck up his right sleeve is a hidden Ace. The pull tie on the sleeve of his leather is a die. Flowing out of his pocket are several chips. I checked with the Pioneer casino and the blue and white ones are the largest they

Great shots of an old cowboy. Notice the shadows on the ground and the horse.

have, $500 each. Jeannie is also packing a derringer in her left pocket. There was a nice shadow and reflection in the gas tank of the bike and it proved to be a perfect spot for an old western train. Items like the train and the derringer are easily found on the Internet and will give you enough of a reference point to paint them accurately. The bike and riders were coming along well, but I was kind of putting off the cowboys in the background. I don't know anything about cowboys so I guess it was kind of a mental block. I did know that if I painted in the wrong type of horse, guns, or clothing, someone would call me on it.

Once again, things fall into place. This probably happens because I take time on my artwork. This painting took me three months to complete. While I'm working on a painting I'm always thinking about future projects and am lining up reference material for those as well. My camera is always with me and I take thousands of photographs. Mom came in to town from Chicago and we decided to take a road trip with her and the kids. We headed for

a day to Nogales, Mexico and were then going over to Tombstone, Arizona to spend the night. I'd never been to Tombstone but I like the movie. Pat and Brooke Kennedy, famed chopper builders, live there so it had to be a cool place. While in Nogales we picked up several bottles

How the hell did those women wear all that clothing in the Tombstone heat?

of Almondjaero. It's almond flavored Tequila they don't sell in the states and it goes down really smooth. While enroute to Tombstone we got on the phone and found a bed and breakfast for the night. It was a nice little house right off the main drag with some cool locals owning it.

As it turned out they were decorating a float for a parade the following day to celebrate some local Wild West days. Suzanne and I introduced them to Almondjaero, both bottles, and they enlightened us about the Tombstone culture, cowboys, horses, and all the items missing in my paintings. It was also a full moon, and Suzanne and I had the opportunity to do some market research. We decided to get the whole "Wild West" experience and took a walk (stumble) down main street Tombstone, armed with our friend Almondjaero, full moon, after midnight. It was awesome, just like the movie, and gave me a vision of what it was like in those days. Or so I thought at the time. The following morning the parade went down Main Street in full regalia. I was able to get reference photos of horses, cowboys, gunslingers, gals, and stagecoaches. I never realized the wheels on the front of a stage-coach are smaller in diameter than the ones on the back. Or the fact that they used Clydes-dale horses to pull the stagecoaches. That's not what they show in the movies.

Cowboys. Change the hat to a do-rag, and put them in a leather jacket, and they'd look like bikers.

110

Thanks to our friends in Tombstone, whatever their names were. We headed back to Phoenix with a hangover and all the accurate photos I needed to complete my painting.

I positioned my cowboys within the painting, kind of checking out the bikers as they pull out of town. The stagecoach is pulling in and horses are rearing back. You'll also find the madam and her co-workers up on the casino balcony. You know, after the Tombstone experience, maybe there are some similarities between the modern day biker and the old west cowboy. The last details were to add the rocks on the ground. To create distance they are clearer and more in focus up front, and vanish in the dust to the distance. I did a dry brush technique over the gravel to create a dusty background effect and give the painting some motion.

The original painting sold immediately and I've reproduced the work in two different size prints. I've received some feedback from several customers that my prints are too large so I decided to try some smaller sizes. Living on the west coast most of the houses are newer and have tall ceilings and big walls. I've forgotten how it was in the Midwest with smaller rooms and hallways. I don't know how this will work out, but it's always a tough decision as to how large to reproduce the print image.

"Gettin' Lucky" in its infancy. I moved around a lot on this work, building it up in layers until it was complete.

"Up-Late" is kind of an odd perspective. You never know if an idea is going to work unless you push the envelope.

Chapter Thirteen

Up Late

Only the Real Bikers Understand

"Up-Late" is one of those magical motorcycle moments only experienced by riders. One of those little motorcycle nuances that often go overlooked because you have been doing them for so long. People who don't ride can't understand this painting. How many times have you gone out riding with the best intention of getting home before dark? Something happens, you meet old friends, you end up somewhere and all of a sudden it's dark out and you forgot your clear glasses for night riding. Your options are: A. Follow that car's taillights in front of you while wearing your dark shades. B. Wear your shades on the edge of your nose while looking over the top of the glasses and put up with your eyes watering. I usually opt for option B, as you can't trust the car and driver in front of you with option A. "Up-Late" is a little whimsical riding paint-ing, a view over the handle-bars, where the rider has for-gotten his clears and has to get home. As usual, I hid a lot more in the painting, but I'll get to that. One of the first exhibits where I showed "Up-

Late" was at the world famous Barrett-Jackson auto auction. Probably 10% of the crowd rides while the majority of the spectators are exotic and classic car people. It was very interesting to watch the car folk observe this work. They tried to understand but just didn't get it. Think about it, it's getting dark out, I'll take off my shades and throw them on the dash of my Lexus. They've never experienced this situation that has happened to me frequently.

"Up-Late" was going to be a hard one to pull

Bikes lined up, and a night street scene from Deadwood, South Dakota, are some of the important elements that make this painting work.

113

off. It was an odd perspective. Put your glasses on the edge of your nose and look over the bars. How would you paint that and what do you see? So, armed with the concept I started to fill in the details. First, I began to gather the reference material. I needed a background with bikes, because after all this was a motorcycle painting. You weren't going to see much of the bike that was being ridden. I was heading to Sturgis so I thought I'd get the reference photos while I was there. I decided on the town of

Deadwood, right outside of Sturgis. Deadwood is an awesome little gambling town that's been refurbished over the years. It's got some interesting buildings and a cool brick street that gets very slippery when wet. During the Black Hills Rally they allow motorcycle parking on one side of the street. I needed a night scene but if I photographed the street scene at night I'd never be able to see the details of the buildings. I figured out what time the sun set and planned to be in Deadwood just before sunset.

Big Joe's arms photographed over his shoulder in my driveway. This is the second time I've used this angle, the first was in "Crank' n."

Walking up and down the sidewalks I found an angle that would work and walked out in the middle of the street. You can get away with stunts like this at motorcycle events because there are photographers and magazine people everywhere taking pictures. I hung out in the middle of the street and took the same angles of photographs over a half hour as the sun set. This gave me a sequence of photographs that I could analyze going from sunset to total darkness. The earlier photographs contained the details of the buildings I needed, the darker ones showed the lighting of the street lamps and lights from the buildings. Back in the studio I used these to pencil in my street scene and establish my lighting.

The arms used in this painting came from a biker I met in a shop. Joe spends a lot of time in the gym and is a cage-fighting champ. He also runs apes on his bike, so we arranged for a time to photograph his arms with hands on the bars. I had Joe sit on his bike like he was riding with his head cocked over to the side. I then shots some pictures with the camera placed where his head would be. These gave me the correct positioning of the bike within the painting. I later photographed Performance Machine controls and levers to draw in to the

114

painting, as I didn't like the look of the stock controls. My friends at KD sunglasses gave me an assortment of colored glasses to work from. I drew these in to the painting, positioning them as if they were on the edge of my nose. Part of the challenge here was how they would fit in the painting and what you would see. If you put glasses on the edge of your nose, do you see your nose? I would have to use some artistic license here to combine the background, arms, bars, glasses, and gas tank. Hold your arms out like they are on handlebars and notice how your arms get blurry or fade away as they approach your shoulders. I decided on a black shirt and black tank to blend the elements together towards the bottom of the painting. Of particular note here is that I didn't get this portion of the painting correct the first time. The tank was painted several different colors, and the whole section of the painting was done several times before I was comfortable with the look I wanted. That's one of the reasons I prefer to work with acrylic paints, they dry fast and can be painted over when you screw up, or don't get the look you're after.

I worked in and out on this painting, moving around the canvas more than usual to accomplish what I set out to do. At certain angles, with specific shades, you get a reflection of your eye in the glasses. I thought that would be an interesting addition and set out to add in some eyeballs. Now I'm pretty good at painting human figures, but had never painted a close up of an eyeball. I checked around the house

and ended up with one of the wife's little make-up mirrors. I held the mirror up close to my left eye and sketched what I saw out of my right eye. So Suzanne comes home from work and sees her make-up shit all over the studio and says, "what the hell are you up to now?" As she puts it, being married to an artist is never boring. I painted in the eyeballs and added some water droplets coming out the sides as if your eyes are watering. The painting was starting to come together at this point and it took a subtle little change. Not only was this a painting about a rider who's forgotten his clears, but I decided to incorporate all the little background items an observant motorcycle rider has to comprehend. You only have a fraction of a second to make a decision on a bike, and I thought it would be interesting to add in those background elements.

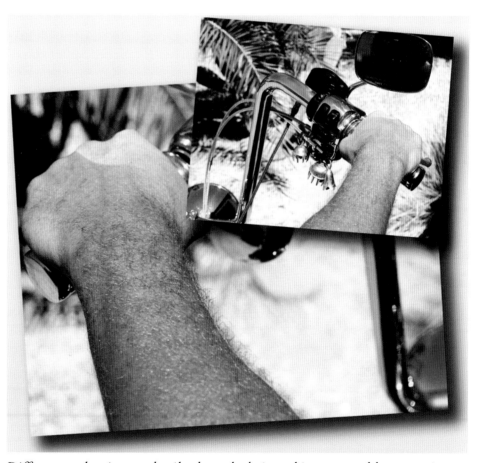

Different angles give me details about the hair on his arms, and how to paint the knuckles and bone structure.

The "Up-Late" rider has his glasses on his nose and his eyes are watering. If you look in his rear view mirror you'll notice his reflection with his blond passenger on the back. In the upper left windows above the pool hall is a naked figure. Walking towards the pool hall are a gal and guy with a pool cue. On the right is a bar with a large bouncer out front. A selection of people walking down the street on the right are having fun and copping a feel. The rider is looking for a parking space, but there doesn't seem to be any as he approaches the party at the end of the street. Nice little street rod heading the other way. Out in front are a chopper and an antique bike. All of these elements are noticed by the "Up-Late" rider in a fraction of a second. That's what makes a good motorcyclist, observation and timing.

Outside of the obvious challenges - like the perspective, this painting contains some tricky little areas. The block wall on the right was very time consuming, as was the street. The blocks are not perfect and had to be painted randomly. The light-ing on the wall also fades from light to dark going left to right. I probably spent two days on the wall. My original intention was to have two ladies of the evening leaning against the brick wall. After the wall was completely painted in, and the painting was near completion, I penciled them in using white pencil. I found they detracted from the painting and drew your attention toward the figures instead of down the road where I wanted the viewer to look. The main focus of this work had to be looking down the street, with small glances off to the left and right. The perspective of the bricks on the road was also tough as they diminished in the distance and in the shadows off to the sides. I painted in the bricks completely before I went to the purple of the shades. I then selected a color that was transparent and thinned it down with water considerably to paint in the purple of the shades. This left the texture of the road through the shades. I later went back in and refined some of the bricks. As I mentioned earlier, this painting was completed by working in and out. Every painting takes a different sequence to complete. It's like starting a kick start bike. If you know the sequence - choke, gas, three turns of throttle, top dead center, kick like hell, and it fires. Every painting has a sequence to completion. If you can figure it out early in the painting it will be completed faster and easier. Otherwise, you'll kick like hell until it's eventually completed. The result may be the same, but you'll get there faster, and easier, if you understand no two paintings are completed in the same sequence and you have to figure it out.

I didn't care for the stock handlebar switches or mirror so I went over to Performance Machine and photographed one of their display bikes. This is also a good way to make friends within the industry.

116

The sky was painted black in the center, thinning out as it approached the buildings. I then laid down several washes of translucent blue over the black. I liked the way the sky turned out as it gets more color closer to the buildings. Stars were added in randomly to the sky, and here you have to watch that they don't look too hokey. Check out some stars at night. Some are bright and in focus, others are blurry, large and small, there are all kinds randomly thrown into a night sky. The lighting of the street scene was also a challenge. In most paintings you will have a single light source on the objects of interest. Like the sun shining down on a bike. In "Up-Late," the light sources are varied and come from street lights, buildings, and head lights. I intentionally enhanced, or brightened up, the lights to give the painting a more dramatic effect. Notice the details at the top of the buildings are lighted from the bottom. Shadows are cast upwards and out in to the street at the same time. The street is lighted in front of the rider from his headlight. I didn't have any reference photos to show off the lighting so I just had to figure out where the highlights and shadows would be cast. It was kind of fun and different from most of my other paintings.

At the bottom of the painting I chose to blend the arms into a black T-shirt and black gas tank. The tank was given just enough definition by adding some white highlights and the blue and purple pin stripping. Subtle things like using the same blue in the pin-stripping, street rod, and the sky, will tie the painting all

together. The purple is the same color used in the glasses, only a different shade with some white mixed in. Glance around the painting and notice where all the blues appear. They may seem random, but the placement of colors was very calculated. This creates harmony and eye movement within a work.

Upon finishing "Up-Late," I carefully took a damp rag with a little dishwashing soap and wiped down the painting. This removes any of the grease pencil marks from the drawing and also removes any loose paint, hairs, or dirt within the paint that may fall off later. I also turn the canvas around and shine a light on the painted surface, looking at the blank side of the canvas. Any areas of the canvas that don't have paint, or that I may have missed, will allow the light to shine through. I go back and touch up these areas, add some highlights, and generally tweak the finished product until it meets my approval. I then coat the canvas with a protective UV coating. These coatings come in a spray can from any art store, and are available in different formats. Depending upon

A close up shows how the brick pattern continues through the glasses. It all has to work together, and sometimes you don't get it right the first time.

117

the painting, I may use a matte finish or a gloss. Anytime you spray something, several thin coats are always better than one thick one. Take some care in coating the finished product and turn the canvas several times so you don't get lines of spray marks running across the painting. A quick note on coating your canvas: have it professionally photographed before you spray on the coating. Sometimes, when photographed, reflections coming off of the canvas will appear as little white marks or stars on the photographs of the painting. I've found these marks show up more when a painting has a gloss finish than when it doesn't. Try to coat your paintings as the last step before they go out to be framed.

While I've changed names to protect the innocent I've also added details where I see fit. Notice the words "Samson building" on the brick building halfway up the street. I exhibit at the Samson building when I'm at Sturgis.

I may as well give you my thoughts on framing a painting as well. When I began painting I used to paint all the way around the edges of the canvas. This gave the work a clean, finished look, and I didn't have to buy a frame. This works better on more contemporary artwork (bold colors and graphics) than intricate pieces. I did this for a while until I made some more money, and my paintings began selling for more. I then decided to start framing them and was glad I did. If you invest $500 in a frame for your painting, it could look like it's worth $5000 more. Paintings always look better framed, period. The risk here is the buyer may not like the frame you have chosen. They may have a specific location in mind to hang the work, but decide the frame doesn't go with their décor. I've spoken to a number of art gallery owners on this subject and they prefer to frame most of their artwork in black frames. This gives the work a finished look but doesn't detract from the painting. Most of my paintings look good in black frames and it is a color of choice for most bikers. Over the years though, I look at my work when it's on display and all of the frames are the same, black. I've intentionally tried to mix up my framing over the years to show customers the different options available. Now, being an artist, you would think I'd be pretty good at selecting the right frame for a painting I have just completed. I suck at it! I've re-framed the same painting several times because of the wrong selection on my part. Over the years I've found a local framer who is very good at what he does, and gives me a fair price because of the volume of my work. Dan will make framing choices for me that I never think will work - and they are usually better than what I would pick. He selects the frame based upon the painting, not on where he thinks it will be hung. Find a good framer and trust their opinions, you will be pleasantly surprised at the outcome.

While I'm on the subject of "Up-Late" and the town of Deadwood, I've got to relay a riding experience I had there. It was one of the best rides I've ever had and my motor wasn't even running! Tom Motzko, a buyer for Drag Specialties, Kenny Price, from Samson Exhaust, and I were riding through Deadwood. Tom asked if I had ever been to Wild Bill Hickock's grave, it's right outside of town. So Kenny, Tom, and I ride up this very steep mountain road to the grave site. It wasn't a long road, but probably a 10% grade. We did the tourist thing, checked out the cemetery, very cool, hand carved stones, and got a little culture while we were in town. As we were leaving Tom says, "now you have to go down the hill with your motor off." Kenny says, "How about we race down?" Tom was riding his very trick FXR, Kenny on a custom bagger built by Jesse James that I now own, and I'm on my custom softail that Harold Pontarelli built. Off we go pushing like Fred Flintstone to get the lead. Kenny on the bagger has the downhill weight advantage and takes the lead as we hit the first corner at about 20 MPH. The trick here is not to hit the brakes or you'll lose momentum, but Tom and I got tight in the first corner and had to tap them. Now it's Kenny in front, I'm number two, and Tom's a close third. We're weaving corners with no brakes and starting to hit speeds up to 45 MPH. As we near town there are parked cars on the left and one of those tourist trolley buses going in the same direction as us down the hill. Kenny, in the lead, has to make a decision on whether he can pass the bus in time before encountering the approaching parked cars. There wasn't enough room to get between the bus and the cars, and you

didn't have a throttle to work, so it was all timing and judgment. Kenny decides to go for it, to take the sure win and squeaks through with probably only an inch on each side of the bagger. He thought he had a sure win knowing no one else would fit through, but didn't check his mirror as I was three inches behind him. My Softail was slimmer than the bagger so I just squeaked through and Tom had to hit the binders. Kenny and I blew past the startled trolley driver, turned on the ignition, banged it in second gear, and dumped the clutches to fire the bikes. What a ride! Even though Kenny won, it was one of the most exciting races of my life, with the motor off. They have since put up a stop sign so you can't run the whole downhill, but it's still an annual ride to the top whenever we're in Dead-wood. Check it out, if not on that hill, try it on another. I'm still trying to figure out how I can put that experience down on canvas. Thanks for the ride Tom and Ken.

"Up-Late" framed and in my studio. The frame works perfectly with this painting and I enjoy elements that are painted oversize. The arms and glasses have a visual impact because they are larger than life.

Chapter Fourteen

Behind Bars

Motorcycle Moments

It's kind of funny how an idea strikes you. The influences for the concept may have been around you for quite some time, and then they just pop up and you need to do a painting of

Part of being an artist is attempting to do something new, a view that you may have seen but has never been put down on canvas. I hope most of my artwork is in that category. I'm sure "Behind Bars" is.

that idea. This is one of those paintings. I also feel it's one of "those motorcycle moments" that riders do so frequently they go unnoticed. There are certain situations that happen only to motorcycle riders that the general public never understands. Having sat in bars for over 30 years now I'm familiar with the drill. You frequently go to the window to check on your bike. You intentionally park the scooter in front of the window so you can keep an eye on it. You never do that with your truck! So I'm sitting in a bar outside Milwaukee (we called it the Black Hole) and I look out the window and think, "what an awesome painting." I was there for Harley's 95th celebration. Kenny and the crew from Samson Exhaust and I were relaxing after a long day. The bar was curved, but if I leaned over I could check on the bikes. I think I had to look around Kenny. Kenny has several decades worth of tattoos, which as an art form I also find very interesting. No ink on me, so I'm kind of intrigued by them and how they change over time. I was also thinking that I don't recall any fine artwork showing tattoos. I've got the basis for a painting, a tattooed arm, looking out

of a bar window, neon sign, and a bunch of bikes in the parking lot. A good thought for a painting. I'm sure it would get refined as I progressed. I've noticed over the years that my paintings and prints don't sell as well if there are people in the work. Was this because people

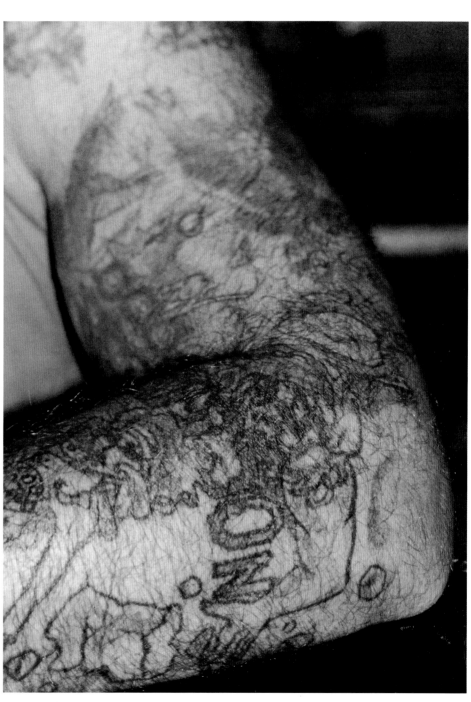

Kenny, from Samson Exhaust, loaned me his arm and educated me about ink work.

don't want to purchase a work of art with someone else's face on it? Maybe I'd try this one with just figures, and no faces, and see how it sells.

The concept for "Behind Bars" became a reality in June. I wanted to use Kenny's arm and wouldn't see him again until November during The Love Ride. After the event Suzanne and I went over to Samson to photograph his arm. Kenny enlightened me about tattoos and

explained how older ones fade out and are not as sharp as recent ink. I took the shots and we headed back to Phoenix. The next step was to get a bar scene. Riding out to my favorite watering hole I lined up some photographs. The bartender, Jeannie, has been used in several of my paintings and I refer to her as my hair and butt model. The only angle that would work for this painting was if I was behind the bar. "Behind Bars" is bartender's perspective of what's going on. Interesting. I took the bar scenes, shot several rolls of Jeannie and photographed the most perfect beer I've ever seen. Sometime later I also photographed a grouping of bikes at The Hideaway.

Armed with my reference materials I returned to the studio. Penciling the idea in took quite awhile and I paid particular attention to the tattoos. Painting the human figure is one of the hardest things to render. The close ups of Kenny's arm appeared to me like layers upon layers. I roughed in the background to establish my color scheme, (which was mostly dark) and immediately went to the tattooed arm. Painting flesh tones and human figures is one thing I think I excel at. For this I give credit to Bob O'Malley, an illustration teacher I had in college. Beginning with the arm, I painted it as I normally would. There are a lot more colors that make up flesh tones than you would realize. They include indigo orange, acra violet, and dark greens and purples in the shadows. Most airbrush artists who paint figures get the smooth shad-

Several shots of my hair and butt model. Notice one of prints hanging on the wall of The Hideaway, a favorite local watering hole.

ing and curves of the human figure, but limit themselves to only a few colors. There is a lot of color in the human figure, and the tattoos added to that. I worked the arm up in layers, moving to the tattoos after the skin tones and shadows were 90% complete. Starting with the oldest and most faded tattoo I moved toward the clarity of the recent ink. Kenny's arm would also be the closest subject to the viewer and had to be painted with the most clarity. After painting in the tattoos I moved to the hair follicles. Notice how they are dark against the skin but light is reflected off of them against the dark background. When the arm was almost complete I went back in and added some highlights from a light source. These highlights would lighten up not only the skin tones, but also the turquoise greens of the ink work. Several additions were made to Kenny's arm, including the removal of several ex-wives names and the replacement of his kid's names. I also added "Laughlin 99" as this was to be the official painting for The Laughlin River Run.

Moving to the bikes next, I created a scene with several bikes in a row. These were painted with a modest degree of detail as they would appear in the distance. I also knew that at a later point in time many of the bikes would be covered up by the neon sign I was going to hang in the window. I did pay attention to the models of bikes and the colors. The pink Heritage is obviously the gals,

while the tattooed biker must be riding the flamed shovelhead. The bikes were photographed during the day so I could see the details, but I made it an evening scene.

Jeannie is a joy to paint. I know why artists have favorite models because some are just more interesting than others. Guys like big hair and a nice butt. Jeannie has both. I set her in a pose

Photographs of the perfect beer are making me thirsty. It's actually a non-alcoholic beer, as the bartender informed me they have a foamy head.

123

leaning on a pool queue against a chair. There wasn't much skin tone to contend with but the hair and jeans would take some time. I started the hair with some large brushes and large areas of color. Her hair was very dark at the top and picked up highlights at the bottom when it reached the curls. Just like the hair on Kenny's arm, there is almost a halo of color and light around the top of her head. Decades ago I was a sign painter and pin striper. I broke out the old striping brushes and cleaned them thoroughly. I was going to try to use them with my acrylic, water based paints instead of the oil-based paints they were designed for. Striping brushes are long and have a lot of hair so they

carry paint for a long time. Long lines can be accomplished with a single stroke, and smooth curves can be painted without lifting your brush from the canvas. I had to keep the paints thin because acrylics tend to dry fast and can ruin a brush or not flow correctly. I worked on Jeannie's hair using probably fifteen colors, over and over, layer upon layer. There was finally a point where I had to stop, but I did have the feeling that I would want to try this hair thing again. I now pay special attention to a woman's hair and how I would paint it. There's a particular red head out there, you know who you are, and I will paint your hair someday.

I've painted enough leather in my time and

Bikes lined up at The Hideaway on a Saturday afternoon. I love this job!

this was no big deal. The difference in rendering leather is whether it's new or old. New has a blue shine to it, where old leather that's worn shows the yellow and gold of the hide. Don't overlook the details like the rock I stuck in her boot. Jeans are always a challenge and these were no different.

Selecting the correct shade of blue seems to be very important here. I chose a blue with more purple in it than green. Try to create some texture and analyze the fabric. Look at a pair of jeans through a magnifying glass and see how the weave is created. It was important here to create some shape and wrinkles in the fabric, while still keeping them tight fitting to show off Jeannie's shape. I particularly like the area around her waist where the jeans become loose and leave a shadow. The red label on the jeans was my own brand and reads "Bite Me."

We've all seen a glass of beer, but did you ever look at one and figure out how to paint it? Within the glass there were layers, bubbles on the outside, the glass, beer inside, and shadows and reflections on the back side. I broke it down to large areas of color - dark browns, gold's,

middle tones, and then started to work toward the details. I knew I could paint the foam as I had mastered the technique of painting bubbles on my painting "Wash Day." The shine of the glass has a certain texture, similar to chrome but a little more random. It took some time,

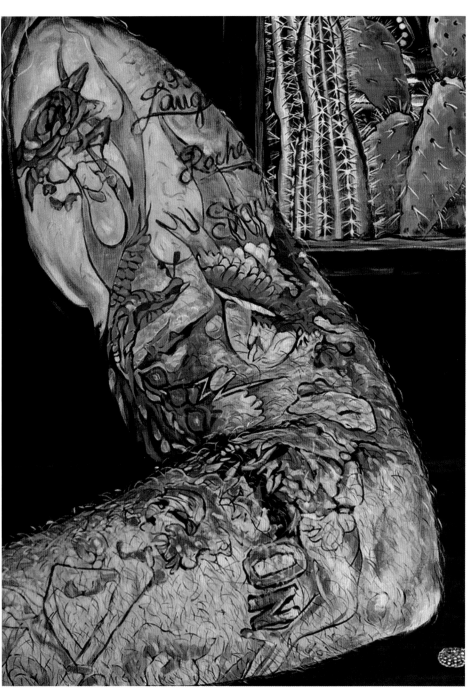

Kenny's arm becomes a painting. Challenging, very challenging. I'll paint some more tattoos in the future. It was cool.

but I got it. I'd like to paint some more glass objects in the future. The foam was a study in highlights and shadows. Creating the craters on the top I stuck with only two colors, black and white. As the bubbles wrap around the side of the glass I've added some gold tones as the foam thins out and you pick up some of the color of the beer.

After the beer it was time to add in the neon sign. Since this was the official painting for 'The Laughlin River Run' I decided to use a place we hang out in Laughlin, The Rainbow Bar. The Rainbow doesn't look anything like this but I'd use the name. I took some photos of neon signs in reverse to see what they looked like. At my drawing table I designed the Rainbow Bar sign and figured out how the tubes would be bent. There's also a metal structure that holds the sign that you only see from the inside of the window. Neon has a particular glow and this is the first time I've painted it. I'd like to try it again against a plain background. Whenever I added more glow to the sign it started to detract from the bikes. Sometimes you have to find a happy medium.

Laughlin is a gambling town so I wanted to round out this work with gambling influences. The slot machine in the background was fun to paint. The round rollers are the lightest in the distance and dark in the front. The light source for these is inside the machine.

The perfect beer - free and cold. The bubbles on top appear as craters with the bubble rising out of the crater. I've got the bubbles down after painting "Wash Day".

126

Jeannie's shoulder crops off the corner so you can't tell if the Jackpot has been hit. The chips on the bar are $100s, because she is obviously high maintenance. There's a set of spurs on the wall that my friend Buzz loaned me. They actually have a gambling motif with hearts, clubs, spades and diamonds on them. In 1998, at Laughlin, there was a grasshopper plague. When I pulled in to town that year bikes were sliding off the road on dead grasshoppers. They were everywhere, even in the salad bar at the hotel. In memory of 1998 I hid some grasshoppers on top of the cactus. I also hid a few dolphins because my friend Dolphin John came up with the title. Now if you were a dolphin, where would you be? I couldn't make it that obvious, but you're probably close.

One last item of note to artists: my wife kept saying as I painted this, "who's going to buy that?" I said every biker with a bar in his garage or basement. While I value her opinion it's nice to prove her wrong occasionally. The prints of "Behind Bars" are a consistent good seller and the original sold immediately, and is in the collection of Kenny Price. My point is,

don't worry about sales. I know it's important, but just paint what you feel like. I learned a lot in this work and will try some of the objects again. Bike styles may come and go, making some of motorcycle art trendy, but I think the behind bars scene will be around awhile.

The details in Jeannie's hair shows skills I learned years ago with my pin stripping brush. If you look closely the hang tag on her jeans reads Bite Me.

Chapter Fifteen

The Unauthorized 100

Harley's 100th Anniversary Party

Well, it's getting closer, Harley's 100th anniversary. I've only had five years to ponder this painting, ever since the 95th. I still don't have a solid idea. I knew I wanted to do something involving the town of Milwaukee and the riders. After all the riders are what helped Harley-Davidson get down the road for 100 years. I grew up in Chicago and was familiar with Milwaukee, and the beautiful Wisconsin countryside. How was I going to capture everything I wanted in this new painting? I'd been to Harley's 90th and 95th celebrations. What made this event different from

The 100 burned out in the pavement is very obvious to me because I painted it. It always amazes me how some people can see things and others don't understand, even after you explain them. I guess that's what makes the world go around.

the other twenty bike events I attend a year? Wherever you go, whether it's Sturgis or Daytona, some of the locals like the bikes, some don't. When in Milwaukee, it seems like all the locals are welcoming the bikers. That was the difference! Riding in to Milwaukee everyone lined the bridges to welcome you there. Kind of an awesome feeling after getting shut out of places because you ride a motorcycle. That's what I needed to portray. The party. The Midwestern hospitality. Now all I had to do was tie that visual in with something that reflected Harley's 100 years. I went around and around and in a conversation with a sculptor friend, Mark Patrick, we came up with the idea of doing a burnout in a 100 configuration. Mark and I went even further and he decided to do a sculpture in his vision, while I did a painting in mine. Two artists, similar ideas, different medium. Cool.

The first step was to figure out the angle of the bike doing the burnout. This was to be the central focus of the painting. I needed to put this in the foreground so I'd have room for a Wisconsin scene behind. I went to the kids' room, a constant reference source, and found a small model of a dirt bike. I took the model, a piece of paper, and a marker, and did some different burnout configurations in the shape of a 100. The 100 was too wide and the bike would have to be small. After playing with this for a

My friend Bill, with his beautiful Shovelhead, posed for the burnout photos. He just completed an old-school Panhead chopper I need to check out for a potential new work.

while I decided to overlap the zeros to compact things a little. This seemed to work so I shot some photos and went to the next level. An important note here is: I try to make the motorcycle occupy at least 25% of the total canvas space. If the bike becomes too small a part of the overall image, then the focus is not on the bike. These are paintings about motorcycles, after all. I've got the angle, now I need the bike.

I wanted a harder core image for this one. You would only see a seasoned rider attempting this stunt. My friend Bill had an outstanding 1968 Shovelhead. This was the last year of Harley-Davidson's ownership before being sold to AMF. Bill's Shovel won the Del Mar Concours de Elegance in 1996, best of show. Great job on the restoration Bill. He has since put on some "apes" and a solo seat and the bike fit the painting perfectly. I took the original layout photos of the burnout, rode over to Bill's, and set him up out in the street. Decked out in his old leathers, in 100 degree Phoenix heat, we staged the shoot. Care was taken at this point to make sure the hand controls were in the correct position. Throttle on, front brake held, clutch out. I screwed up on a few details, but had Bill over to the house before the painting went out the door and he caught the mistakes. Little stuff, but very important. We had the fuel petcock off when originally photographed and I painted it that way at first. It's all in the details. If you're going to paint bikes, then you'd better know them and

Photographs of some clouds vanishing in to the distance will work as a good reference for this painting.

ride them. Someone would have caught the pet-cock error and there goes my credibility. I can screw up on my own, I try not to do it in my art-work. There were a few clouds going overhead that day and I made some observations. The chrome and sheet metal looked better with the clouds reflected in them, but the shadows and the details of the bike looked better in bright sun. I shot photos from the exact same angles with, and without, the clouds. I used several photos combined to get what I needed in the finished painting.

Some of the other reference photos taken include the burnouts and the chopper blasting by. As images in the distance of the painting become less focused, reference materials become less

important. Most of the scenery, trees, buildings, and exit ramp were made up from memory. The burnouts were important because I was working with a forced perspective on this work. I had to create the illusion of a great distance in a small amount of space. I knew of a street near the local bike shop where a lot of rubber was laid down on the ground. Once again, off with the camera to figure out how to paint a burnout. Examining the burnouts, I noticed a lot of layers. There were some dark marks on top of other older patches. I learned this trick painting technique years ago and also used it on my Laughlin River Run painting. Taking the canvas I laid it horizontal, parallel to the ground. I took a level and made sure it was flat. Armed with a box of kosher rock

I needed a chopper for the background so I went over to Hacienda Customs and photographed this Big Dog. People are more than willing to help an artist if you're courteous and don't take to much of their time.

salt, my paints, a hair dryer, and plenty of water, I got to work. First I soaked the canvas leaving puddles of water on top. Next I started to add some color to the asphalt in the puddles of water. The paint thins and spreads in the water and I applied darker lines in the areas of the burnouts. Before the water dried I applied a sprinkle of the rock salt. Then taking a hair drier, I dried up the excess water. After completely dry (five minutes) I took the straight edge of a ruler and scraped off the rock salt. The rock salt will soak up the water and also the paint pigment. It leaves little pebble like marks that resemble the texture of asphalt. Taking all afternoon, I repeated this step probably ten times using slightly different colors. I used watered down colors that were going to be used in the background, blues, greens, golds and purples. The combination of these pastel colors in layers created an interesting shade of grey. I had also built the pavement up in layers, and created the effect of burnout on top of burnout. Some patch-outs were made darker and more prominent than others. The colors and texture of the rock salt created a random interesting pattern that resembled asphalt. I sprinkled more rock salt in the foreground of the painting than in the distance. This started to give the painting some depth as the details diminish in the distance. I went in later and added more pebble texture one rock at a time where needed, but using this technique I painted in 90% of the road in an afternoon. It's also one of those techniques where

There just happens to be a street I know where bikers like to practice their burnouts. These photos saved me a tire as I first thought I'd have to create these myself.

other artists and observant people will get three inches away from the canvas and think, how did he paint in all those little rocks. Tricks of the trade.

The bike's penciled in, I've got the asphalt 90% complete, and the background blues of the sky are established, as well as the green farmland. I started to move around at this point, filling the painting with visual Wisconsin landmarks. It's not necessary to have perfect reference material for background items, but try to draw a tractor from memory. The Internet has become a valuable tool for an artist. If you're just looking for angles, and some basic reference, everything you may need is there. The bar was penciled in, as well as the gas station. I began painting small people lining the bridge. At this point I thought, how about putting 100 people in the painting. I began to count the people and added bikes that I would encounter at an event like this. There are always a few riders taking a break under the overpass. Take a closer look and find some flashers and a rider relieving himself. Wisconsin is known for its farms and dairy cows so they became elements as well as a farmer drinking beer. The memorable welcome to Wisconsin with the Milwaukee skyline in the distance. In addition to Harley-Davidsons 100th Anniversary it was also the 100th for Ford Motors and 100 years of aviation. You'll find a '32 Ford High Boy, The Wright Brothers Flyer and some F-18's. There's a lot of truck traffic in the Milwaukee area so we have one entering the

ramp as well. Once again, I used a small model of a truck to get the correct angle.

This was to be a fun painting. All about bikers having fun at an event. The chopper was added, blowing by on one wheel. I rode to a local shop and photographed one at the correct angle. Mistake made here. Don't photograph a black bike for reference. It's hard to see the details. I painted it red in the artwork. By moving around when I was working on this piece I consciously tried to create a consistent flow with the colors. The rider has a red shirt and bandanna, red chopper, red roof on the gas station, red on the American flags on the bridge. It was all coming together, but the focus was starting to be pulled away from the rider doing the burnout. I knew the last item I was going to add would be the smoke from the burnout. I had envisioned the smoke coming off the bike extending to the upper right corner. This would pull your eye in towards the bike, but that would leave the left side of the painting bland. Eye movement around a painting is very important to the finished work.

These miniature motorcycle models are a handy tool to figure out angles and perspectives for potential painting concepts.

Especially in a painting as busy as this one. I decided to put some very strong clouds moving towards the central bike from the upper left. These clouds balanced out the powerful whites of the smoke coming in from the other side. The clouds were painted in a similar style and with the same colors of the smoke. I made the smoke a little looser, as it was moving faster than the clouds, a little more transparent.

Smoke is a tricky subject to paint because it is transparent and dissipates quickly. I painted it several times until I was comfortable with the outcome. It's a little stylized with some tire movement of the bike showing through. Having taken so much time painting the back end of the bike, I didn't want to cover it in smoke. I only had one shot at this. If it didn't work I'd be repainting the back half of the bike. A dry brush technique was used. Some whites and grays were applied to a large brush with no water. Most of the paint was then brushed out of the brush on a palette of paper. Only a slight, almost dry residue of paint was left on the brush. With very even pressure the 'dry brush' was glazed over the sheet metal painting of the bike. Paint was only applied to the top surface texture of the canvas, leaving the blue of the bike to shine through. Dry brush is a tricky technique used by artists and practiced over a lifetime. You only get more consistent with the technique, you never master it. I enjoy it and use this technique wherever a whisper of color is needed. It works well for clouds, smoke, and that

The beginning stages with some of my reference material taped to the top of my canvas. I worked on the road during the entire painting and finally got it right by the time the work was complete.

subtle white highlight you'll find at the edge of chrome in a cloud reflection.

I wanted to title this work to commemorate not only Harley-Davidson's 100th Anniversary, but all things 100 - especially the 100 people in the painting. The "Unauthorized 100" came up because most of the people are doing unauthorized acts. Burnouts, wheelies, flashing - all that harmless, biker fun that happens at an event of this magnitude. I went to the 100th straight from Sturgis during 2003. It was one of the longest stretches I've been on tour, seven weeks out. My assistant Lisa and I had a blast. The people of Milwaukee and the surrounding area couldn't have been nicer. The police were even giving directions instead of tickets. It was a memorable event for me, as I'm sure it was for 300,000 other bikers. I'm glad I portrayed the people in this commemorative painting, because that's what was different about the 100th from all the other events. Thanks to my friends, Jill's in Kenosha (a serious fun biker bar) and Bill for loaning me his condo for free when you couldn't find a room for 100 miles. These are some examples of Midwestern biker hospitality that I'll never forget. Bonus points: the original painting sold before the 100th at Sturgis and is in Racine, Wisconsin in the collection of Dan Bishop. It couldn't be in a better place. Thanks Harley-Davidson. Thanks Milwaukee.

A close up shows how the road was built up in layers. I added in the cracks to create some character.

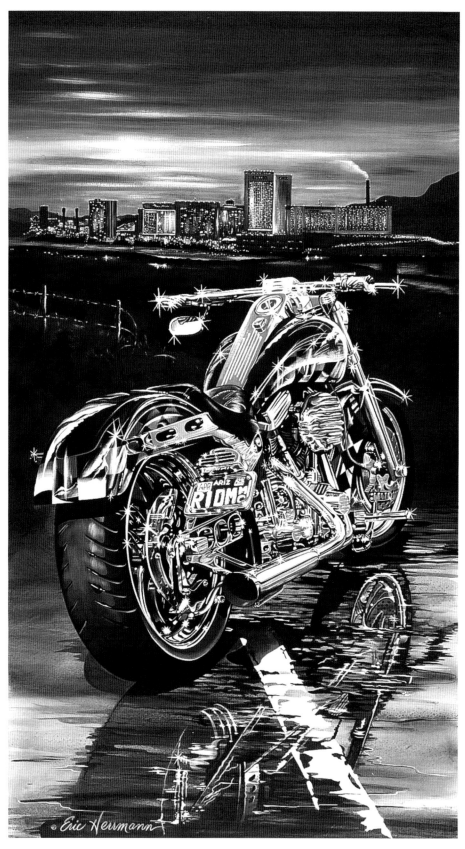

Part of what makes the first "Laughlin" painting a success is something no one but an artist will notice. It's the eye movement around the canvas. It begins with a focus on the bike, then you are drawn down the white stripe to the reflections, and also through the town, and up river to the top left of the canvas.

Chapter Sixteen

Laughlin

A Biker Mecca in the Desert

I've found that change is good for me. Whenever I've decided to make a change in my life, artwork, motorcycles, or whatever, it's been based on calculated decisions and the outcome is usually a better thing. This painting is a prime example. What started out as a motorcycle painting developed into a piece of artwork to commemorate a biking event - The Laughlin River

I hiked up a hill outside of town to get just the right angle to include most of the casinos along the strip. I've been going to Laughlin ever since there were only two buildings.

Run. Changes were made to the original painting, a process that I rarely do, and the outcome was very beneficial.

The original painting was a bike, set in a colorful background, against some distant palm trees. I'd decided I needed to strike up a relationship with one of the big motorcycle rallies and get one of my paintings to be the official artwork. While this has been done before at many sporting events, it had rarely been pulled off for motorcycle events. There is always an official work of art for the Olympics, Indianapolis 500, The Super Bowl, and others. I couldn't recall an official work of art for any of the bike rallies. Maybe it was time. I thought about all the events I attend annually and decided on The Laughlin

River Run. Other events like Sturgis and Daytona Bike Week were larger, but Laughlin had a unique character and was approachable. The other larger events had too much politics and had almost gotten out of hand. Laughlin was also a West Coast event only several hundred miles from home. If I was going to align myself with an event, I decided that I wanted Laughlin.

I set out by hunting down the event promoters and approached them with my idea. I'd create an official painting, let them use it for advertising and other purposes, and we could both benefit. This was early in my career and I needed all the exposure I could get. I was also relatively unknown and it wasn't the easiest sell I've ever had. I worked for months calling these people

While the town is technically correct, I took liberties with the colors and the lights.

138

and was getting nowhere fast. After all, the event had been going on for years, growing all the time. Why did they need me or my artwork? So while I continued to paint, I kept badgering these folks until one day I got a call, and they said "let's do it." The only problem was the event was a month away and it didn't leave me any time to create an original work for Laughlin.

My latest painting contained a purple bike set against a backdrop of palm trees. I had watered down the ground when I photographed the bike so I could get some reflections off the ground - something I had wanted to try for quite some time. I live in the desert and it has a unique character all of its own. When it gets extremely hot the ground will give off a small reflection because of the heat, kind of like a mirage. I decided to alter the original painting and use the water-like reflections to appear as the heat of a desert evening. All I needed to do was drop the Laughlin skyline in the background. I jumped on the scooter and rode over to Laughlin to get some photos. I'd been attending Laughlin for several years and was familiar with the area. As I rode around town looking for the perfect vantage point to capture all of the buildings in the background, one area stuck out in my mind. Laughlin is just across the river from Arizona, which is a no-helmet state. Nevada (Laughlin) requires a helmet. Every time I rode across the river I had to put that damn helmet on. I kept stopping at the same place, right before the

bridge to put on my helmet. It occurred to me that everyone attending Laughlin, entering from the Arizona side of the river, had to do the same thing. All the bikers would have to stop at this vantage point to put on their helmets before crossing in to Nevada. It was the perfect spot. I had a great view of the city of Laughlin, and virtually every biker attending the event has at one point in time stopped there to put on a helmet. I took some photos during the daylight and hauled ass back to the studio to get started.

I whited out the whole top portion of the painting, palm trees and all, and began to pencil in my new background. I used some artistic license here because the photos were taken from the top of a hill, where there is no parking lot. I added in some barbed wire and cactus near the bike to give it a desert feel. As I started to paint I realized I needed to keep the original color scheme of the purples in the sky. The bike was already painted and the chrome was composed of

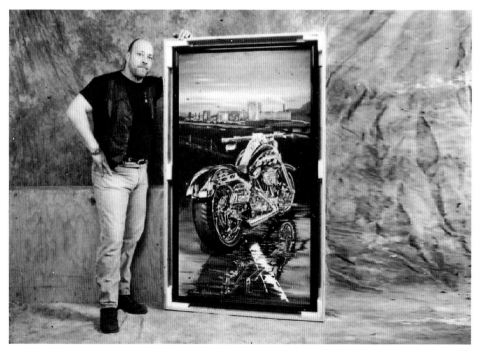

I'm holding the finished Laughlin painting, framed and crated, ready to ship to its new home. Paintings are professionally crated and shipped air freight, heavily insured, to their destination. I've never had any problems, knock on wood.

blues and purples from the original background. Remember, chrome picks up the reflections of its surroundings. I needed to make all the buildings and the sky purple. I was working in reverse, as I usually paint in the background first before the chrome. It took some doing, but I painted in the buildings using mostly purple, and maintained the original color scheme of the painting. Care was taken to maintain the integrity of the skyline, and get all of the casino buildings as accurately as possible. There is also a power plant that is predominant in the Laughlin skyline. The smoke stack was added with smoke forming some white of the night sky.

When the painting was complete, I felt it turned out better than the original work with the palm trees. It appears that the lights from the town of Laughlin are casting the reflections on the pavement from a hot desert evening. I had made a change to a painting that I had spent months on, but it turned out as a better piece. I did have several concerns though: one was the use of all the purple and magenta (pink) in this painting. Was it too feminine? A purple biker painting for my first official Laughlin work? While the desert does appear purple at times, I was still a little worried. After all, this painting was going on the cover of the official program, T-shirts, all that stuff. Was I going to be the biker that did that cute little purple painting?

Reference photos taken behind Myron's, Easyriders of Scottsdale, bike shop. I watered down the ground with a hose to get the look I was after.

This work taught me a lesson. Don't dwell on it or over think your art. Just paint what you want or feel. "The Laughlin River Run" painting sold immediately. The prints are one of my best sellers and as of the writing of this book are almost sold out. The Laughlin promoters loved the outcome of this first official painting, I am now the official artist of The River Run and have created several paintings to commemorate this event. The art has appeared on T-shirts, catalog covers, limited edition prints, and I'm told was appraised on Antiques Road Show. It has been a huge success both financially and promotionally, and I was concerned it was too purple. Shows how much I know. One of the highest compliments I received on this work was from the chapter president of a club in New Mexico. This club member stood in my display at Durango for quite some time, just staring at the painting. He then introduced himself and said he'd never seen the desert painted like that before. He elaborated on how at certain times of the evening the sky and mountains turn to purple on a hot desert evening. He thanked me for creating the painting and said, "keep up the good work." Some of the best rewards are not promotional or financial, but in a small compliment from someone. I remember that moment and conversation like it was yesterday, and I always will.

My rendition of the watered down ground. I enjoy the bald tire on an expensive bike. It shows that he rides the wheels off of it.

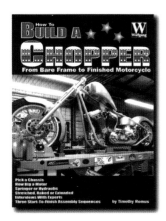

HOW TO BUILD A CHOPPER

Designed to help you build your own chopper, this book covers History, Frames, Chassis Components, Wheels and Tires, Engine Options, Drivetrains, Wiring, Sheet Metal and Hardware. Included are assembly sequences from the Arlen Ness, Donnie Smith and American Thunder shops. Your best first step! Order today.

Choppers are back! Learn from the best how to build yours.
12 chapters cover:
- Use of Evo, TC, Shovel, Pan or Knucklehead engines
- Frame and running gear choices
- Design decisions - short and stubby or long and radical?
- Four, five or six-speed trannies

Twelve Chapters   144 Pages $24.95   Over 300 photos-over 50% color

BUILD THE ULTIMATE V-TWIN MOTORCYCLE

An explosion of new parts from the motorcycle aftermarket now makes it possible to build your own motorcycle from scratch. One designed from the start to answer your need for speed and style. This book is intended to help you make intelligent choices from among the vast number of frames, engines and accessories available today.

You can assemble all those parts into a running motorcycle with tips from men who build bikes professionally. Learn which is the best wiring harness or transmission and the best way to install those parts on your new bike.

After designing, choosing and assembling, all that's left is the registration and insurance. From the first concept to the final bolt, from dream to reality. Yes, you can build your own motorcycle.

Ten Chapters   144 Pages $19.95   Over 250 photos

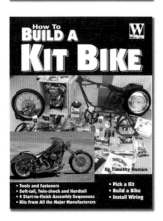

HOW TO BUILD A KIT BIKE

How To Build a Kit Bike explains how to choose the best kit and then assemble those parts into a complete running motorcycle. See bikes built in the shops of: Cory Ness, Kendall Johnson and American Thunder. If you own a kit or plan to buy a kit bike, this is the book you need — designed to help you turn that pile of parts into your own very cool motorcycle.

Eight chapters with 300+ photos & illustrations.
- Tools and Fasteners
- Soft-tail, Twin-shock and Hardtail
- 4 Start-to-Finish Assembly Sequences
- Kits From All The Major Manufacturers

Eight Chapters   144 Pages $24.95   Over 300 photos, 60% color

ADVANCED CUSTOM PAINTING TECHNIQUES

When it comes to custom painting, there is one name better known than all the others, and that name is Jon Kosmoski. Whether the project in your shop rides on two wheels or four, whether you're trying to do a simple kandy job or complex graphics, this how-to book from Jon Kosmoski is sure to answer your questions. Chapters one through three cover Shop Equipment, Gun Control and Paint

Materials. Chapters four through seven get to the heart of the matter with complete start-to-finish painting sequences.
- Shop set up
- Gun Control
- Use of new paint materials
- 4 start-to-finish sequences
- Two wheels or four
- Simple or complex
- Kandy & Klear

Seven Chapters   144 Pages $24.95   Over 350 photos, 100% color

More Great Books From Wolfgang Publications!

http://www.wolfgangpublications.com

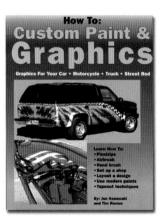

HOW TO: CUSTOM PAINT & GRAPHICS

A joint effort of the master of custom painting, Jon Kosmoski and Tim Remus, this is the book for anyone who wants to try their hand at dressing up their street rod, truck or motorcycle with lettering, flames or exotic graphics. A great companion to Kustom Painting Secrets (below).

7 chapters include:
• Shop tools and equipment
• Paint and materials
• Letter & pinstripe by hand
• Design and tapeouts
• Airbrushing
• Hands-on, Flames and signs
• Hands-on, Graphics

Seven Chapters   144 Pages $24.95   Over 250 photos, 50% in color

KUSTOM PAINTING SECRETS

More from the master! From the basics to advanced custom painting tricks, Jon Kosmoski shares his 30 years of experience in this book. Photos by publisher Tim Remus bring Jon's text to life. A must for anyone interested in the art of custom painting.

7 chapters include:
• History of House of Kolor
• How to set up a shop
• Color painting sequences
• Prepare for paint
• Final paint application
• Hands-on, basic paint jobs
• Hands-on, beyond basic paint
• Hands-on, custom painting

Seven Chapters   128 Pages $19.95   250 photos with color section

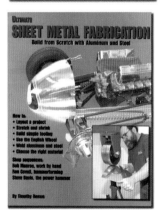

ULTIMATE SHEET METAL FABRICATION

In an age when most products are made by the thousands, many yearn for the one-of-kind metal creation. Whether you're building or restoring a car, motorcycle, airplane or (you get the idea), you'll find the information you need to custom build your own parts from steel or aluminum.

11 chapters include:
• Lay out a project
• Pick the right material
• Shrinkers & stretchers
• English wheel
• Make & use simple tooling
• Weld aluminum or steel
• Use hand and power tools

Eleven Chapters   144 Pages $19.95   Over 350 photos

ADVANCED SHEET METAL FABRICATION

Advanced Sheet Metal Fabrication Techniques, is a photo-intensive how-to book. See Craig Naff build a Rolls Royce fender, Rob Roehl create a motorcycle gas tank, Ron Covell form part of a quarter midget body and Fay Butler shape an aircraft wheel fairing. Methods and tools include English wheel, power hammer, shrinkers and stretchers, and of course the hammer and dolly.

• Sequences in aluminum and steel
• Multi-piece projects
• Start to finish sequences
• From building the buck to shaping the steel
• Includes interviews with the metal shapers
• Automotive, motorcycle and aircraft

7 Chapters   144 Pages $24.95   144 pages, over 300 photos - 60% color

143

Sources

www.ericherrmannstudios.com • (888) 200-6554
42215 N. La Plata Rd. • Cave Creek, AZ 85331

"Unauthorized 100"
25 x 34 Limited Edition of 950
signed & numbered $125.00
Artist Proof (50) $250.00
Canvas Edition (framed) (50) $650.00
30 x 40 Giclee' canvas framed (50) $2500.00

"Wired"
26 x 34 Limited edition of 950
signed & numbered $125.00
Artist Proof (50) $250.00
Canvas Edition (framed) (50) $650.00
30 x 40 Giclee' canvas framed (50) $2500.00

"Dangerous"
27 x 33 Limited edition of 950
signed & numbered $ 125.00
Artists proof (50) $ 250.00
Canvas edition, framed $ 650.00
30 x 40 Giclee' canvas enhanced,
framed (50) $2500.00

"Up Late"
22 x 28 Limited edition of 950
signed & numbered $125.00
Artist Proof (50) $250.00
Canvas edition framed (50) $650.00
30 x 40 Giclee'canvas framed (50) $2500.00

"The Laughlin River Run"
23 x 34 Limited edition of 950
signed & numbered $ 250.00
Artist Proof (50) $500.00
Canvas edition framed (50) $850.00
30 x 40 Giclee' canvas framed (50) $2500.00

"Crank'n"
25 x 34 Limited edition of 950
signed & numbered $ 250.00
Artist Proof (50) $500.00
Canvas edition framed (50) $850.00
30 x 40 Giclee' canvas framed (50) $2500.00

"The Afterburn"
26 x 36 Limited edition of 950
signed & numbered $125.00
Artist Proof (50) $250.00
Canvas Edition framed (50) $650.00
30 x 40 Giclee' canvas framed (50) $2500.00

"Behind Bars"
23 x 29 Limited edition of 950
signed & numbered $ 125.00
Artist Proof (50) $250.00
Canvas edition framed (50) $650.00
30 x 40 Giclee' canvas framed (50) $2500.00

"Wash Day"
27 x 38 Limited edition of 1,500
signed & numbered $ 165.00
Artist Proof (50) $330.00
Canvas Edition (framed) (50) $650.00
30 x 40 Giclee' canvas framed (50) $2500.00

"Gettin' Lucky"
16 x 20 Paper Giclee/Limited Edition
of 300, signed & numbered $125.00
22 x 28 Paper Giclee/Limited Edition
of 300, signed & numbered $350.00
30 x 40 Giclee' Canvas
enhanced framed (50) $2500.00

"Shovelheat"
26 x 30 Limited edition of 950
signed & numbered $ 125.00
Artist Proof (50) $250.00
Canvas Edition (framed) (50) $650.00
30 x 40 Giclee' canvas framed (50) $2500.00

"The King of Flames"
22 x 29 Limited edition of 950
signed & numbered $ 125.00
Artist Proof (50) $250.00
Canvas Edition (framed) (50) $650.00
30 x 40 Giclee' canvas framed (50) $2500.00

"High Noon"
23 x 32 Limited edition of 950
signed & numbered $ 125.00
Artist Proof (50) $250.00
Canvas Edition (framed) (50) $650.00
30 x 40 Giclee' canvas framed (50) $2500.00

"Casino"
23 x 34 Limited edition of 950
signed & numbered $ 125.00
Artist Proof (50) $250.00
Canvas Edition (framed) (50) $650.00
30 x 40 Giclee' canvas framed (50) $2500.00

"Indy 2000"
25 x 39 Limited edition of 950
signed & numbered $ 250.00
Artist Proof (50) $500.00
Canvas Edition (framed) (50) $850.00
30 x 40 Giclee' canvas framed (50) $2500.00

"Outlaw Justice"
18 x 20 Limited edition of 950
signed & numbered $ 95.00
Artist Proof (50) $190.00
Canvas Edition (framed) (50) $650.00
30 x 40 Giclee' canvas framed (50) $2500.00

"Sturgis III, The Canyon Ride"
26 x 30 Limited edition of 950
signed & numbered $ 125.00
Artist Proof (50) $250.00
Canvas Edition (framed) (50) $650.00
30 x 40 Giclee' canvas framed (50) $2500.00

"Billet Proof"
27 x 35 Limited edition of 950
signed & numbered $ 125.00
Artist Proof (50) $250.00
Canvas Edition (framed) (50) $650.00
30 x 40 Giclee' canvas framed (50) $2500.00

"Spike's Garage"
27 x 31 Limited edition of 950
signed & numbered $ 125.00
Artist Proof (50) $250.00
Canvas Edition (framed) (50) $650.00
30 x 40 Giclee' canvas framed (50) $2500.00

"Not Pork"
22 x 29 Limited edition of 950
signed & numbered $ 125.00
Artist Proof (50) $250.00
Canvas Edition (framed) (50) $650.00
30 x 40 Giclee' canvas framed (50) $2500.00

"Barrett-Jackson"
24 x 36 signed open edition $50.00
Canvas Edition Framed (50) $650.00
30 x 40 Giclee' canvas enhanced framed(50) $650.00

"Malibu"
18 x 24 Limited edition of 300 Giclee'
signed & numbered $ 400.00

"Scootin"
Paper Giclee', edition of 300
signed & numbered $400.00

"Wicked"
Limited edition of 300
signed & numbered Giclee' $ 400.00

"Daytona"
Signed Open Edition $ 35.00

"Time Out"
Signed Open Edition $ 35.00

"Gina"
Limited edition of 1,500 signed & numbered and
autographed by Gina, former Ms. Harley-Davidson.
$ 125.00

Collage Poster
23 x 29 Poster $20.0